37 Days

The Disenfranchisement of a Philadelphia Poll Worker

Daryl M. Brooks

Stephen Martino

Courage is an inner resolution to go forward despite obstacles; Cowardice is submissive surrender to circumstances. Courage breeds creativity; cowardice represses fear and is mastered by it. Cowardice asks the question, is it safe? Expediency asks the question, is it politic? Vanity asks the question, is it popular? But conscience asks the question, is it right? And there comes a time when we must take a position that is neither safe, nor politic, nor popular, but one must take it because it is right.

-Dr. Martin Luther King Jr.

CONTENTS

ACKNOWLEDGMENTS
DARYL M. BROOKS

I'd like to first thank my mother, Janie Brooks, and my father, Robert Griffin. I'd also like to acknowledge my children: Dimonique Brooks, Julion Jacobs, Naji Brown, and Iman Sasha Brown Brooks and my grandkids: Malik Bell and Little Janie.

A special thank you goes out to my family in Saint Mary's GA, the Wilsons, the Myers, the Jones and the Johnsons.

A special shout-out to Calvin Poopie Wilson, Artie Jones JR. and son AJ. Derek Smith, Mable "Sista "Johnson, Jaunlette Simmons and family, Kathy McBride and family, Anwar Salandy, Barbara Gonzals and family. Elvis Takar, Nate Jones Jr., Stephen Martino, George Hathaway, Joe Siano, Lou Jasikoff, James White, Steven J. Schmidt, Pastor Greg Locke, Mayor Rudy Giuliani, Corey Lewandowski , and President Donald Trump

I would like to thank my heroes: Dr. Martin Luther king Jr., Dr. Bernard Lafayette, Nate Jones Sr. Rev. S. Howard Woodson, John Watson, Kathy McBride, Father Brian McCormick, Rabbi Gordon Geller, Doc Long, and Mangalisa Davis.

Special thanks go out also to Anwar Salandy for helping to edit this book and to Jaunlette Simmons for taking the cover photo.

PROLOGUE

To me, the 2000 presidential election was more than just a political race between then Governor George W. Bush and Vice President Al Gore. It was political theater at its finest. There was no need to turn on the NBA or see if the Philadelphia Eagles were playing the Cowboys. I had all the excitement I needed right there in Florida. It just wasn't me glued to the TV; it was the whole world watching as lawyers descended on Florida like a bunch of locusts trying to devour as much as they could eat along the way.

Plus, I never heard of such a thing as a "chad" until the 2000 presidential election. The only Chad I knew was this white dude who sat next to me in class. Now, all I heard about day in and day out was about the "chad". There was the "hanging chad" and the "dimpled chad". Hell, there was even the "pregnant chad". What made this political theater even funnier were those guys looking at these chads through big-ass magnifying glasses.

Is this what our democracy had come down to? A bunch of pencil neck suits eye-balling these punch cards as if they were looking at a fine diamond? Hell, I thought I was watching an episode of the 3 Stooges.

Times were different in the year 2000. I was different. Back then, I was a registered Democrat, and a proud one in that. Hell, all of us inner-city African Americans were Democrats. It wasn't a choice or any conscious decision. If you were born in the hood, it made you automatically a Democrat. If you weren't, the guys thought you were some sort of sell-out or "Uncle Tom."

I'm certainly no "Tom" or any kind of sell-out either. However, I always thought for myself and never blindly followed the crowd. Unlike the unusual Democrat from the hood, I was a Blue Dog Democrat- just like all my extended family members down in Georgia. I believed in the second amendment of the US Constitution, God, and most importantly, family. If a guy wants to go out and kill his dinner and come home and cook it up, there's nothing wrong with that. This is America. Live and let live. I don't get into your business, and you don't get into mine.

Though I rooted for Vice President Gore in 2000, I thought the man made some serious mistakes. For one, unlike when running in 1988, he turned away from his Christian base and ran as a more secular candidate. His support for such things as abortion and a strict belief in the separation of church and state just didn't sit well with me.

Also, back then, the Democratic party wasn't like it is now. Gore ran on a platform that promised a balanced budget, strong national defense, and tax cuts. Just look where 20 years took us! The current Democratic party looks nothing like that off 2000 and is a far cry from that of the Kennedy days.

However, the other option in 2000 wasn't that great either. What type of appeal did a governor from Texas have with me or anyone else that came from the hood?

None. Zip. The man had nothing in common with my friends or I, and I didn't want any Texas ranger in the

White House either.

So, on November 7, 2000, I was rooting for a Gore victory.

Little did I know the firestorm that was about to hit the political world that election day. It was like a constitutional tug of war as the electoral college split evenly between my boy Gore and the Texan. It all came down to one state whose ballots had not been fully counted, Florida. Whomever won Florida's electoral votes would win the election.

How does one state end up determining who would become president? One state! And now all eyes were on this state. I never heard of Broward County or Dade County before. But now, that's all they were talking about on the TV. And that's all us common American folk had on our minds.

The funniest thing was that Gore initially called Bush and conceded the race. He then phoned him back 45 minutes later and took it back. I would have liked to hear Bush's reaction. Maybe it went something like, "You got to be kidding me! What are you, some kind of fool or something?"

I thought I was stiffed before. He's like the poor sap standing there all dressed up and alone in his tux while his girlfriend decided to go to the prom with some other dude. Hell. That's being stood up, big league.

Then, all these lawsuits began. By the end of the next day, there were more lawyers in Florida than there were people. Dick Cheney, the Texan's running mate, got so excited about the whole ordeal that he suffered a heart attack. I don't know how many that he had before, but I knew he couldn't have many more before he dropped dead.

They say a cat has 9 lives. If Cheney were a cat, he had to have blown through at least eight by now, and he hadn't

3

even stepped foot in the White House.

The fight between Bush and Gore got so fierce that it went all the way up to the Florida Supreme Court, who allowed the hand count of the ballots in certain counties where there were some inconsistencies. What I didn't understand when I watched the recount was that the ballots were these old-ass punch cards that looked like they came out of some sort of computer museum.

It's the year 2000, man, and here Florida was using these punch cards from the 1960's. Hell, we put a man on the moon and that's the best they could do?

In the end, the US Supreme Court had to put an end to the nonsense going on in Florida. They cited the Equal Protection Clause of the 14th Amendment in order to stop the hand count of votes. They ruled that different counting methods in different counties violated this clause and made the current hand count unconstitutional. I read the clause myself. However, to this day, I still don't know how it applied to what happened in Florida.

However, you know who did understand? Al Gore. After the ruling, he took his himself over to the phone and finally conceded to Bush, giving him the 25 electoral votes to become president. That was December 13, 2000, 37 days after the polls officially closed on November 7th. This time there were no call backs or retractions. Bush was going to the White House, and Gore was now that poor sap left home alone on prom night- just to become some footnote in American history.

Mister "I invented the internet" had finally lost. Maybe if a little of Clinton's personality had rubbed off on him and he didn't distance himself so far away from this notorious womanizer, things would have been a little different.

What was ironic was how the media covered those 37 days from November 7th to Gore's concession. They were thorough and in-depth about everything that was going on. I was glued to the TV the whole time. I knew all of Florida's counties, the lawyers' names, the types of lawsuits that were being filed and counter filed, and the exact vote count, minute by minute. It wasn't until after a fair and thorough coverage of this entire 37-day event that the media officially predicted Bush as the winner.

Hell, contrast that to today. Do you think the mainstream media gives a damn about covering the post-election like they did back in 2000? That's a big, hell no. Instead of reporting the different lawsuits that were being filed, evidence of voter fraud, and the problems with the voting machines, they declared that the old, demented, Uncle Fester look alike, Joe Biden, was the winner. It took them only 4 days, and the recount had not even begun. And if you questioned their conclusion, they called you a right-wing nut, conspiracy theorist, or a racist. Plus, the mainstream media, along with other social media platforms, censored dissenting opinions.

Trump got the short end of the stick. CNN, MSNBC and all of these other mainstream propaganda machines used any excuse they could to declare Biden the winner. There was no fair and balanced reporting. Hell, there isn't any fair and balanced news network left. Even Fox News sold out in the end. Remember the days when the media was honest and provided trustworthy stories?

What got me so angry was the media did nothing at all to cover the massive voter fraud that went on in the election. There was no reporting on the investigations, allegations of fraud, proof of election illegitimacy, or even the ongoing lawsuits filed by Trump and his team. Instead, the media was calling Trump an obstructionist for not allowing Biden to make his transition team.

The truth was that the only thing Joe Biden and his son

should have been transitioning into was the local jail.

Back in 2000, all I heard on the news was how every vote counted and that the legitimacy of the democracy had to be upheld. It was all about the fairness in the votes and how every voice counted. Jump 20 years later to 2020, and none of that mattered any longer. Once the media declared Biden the winner, that was the end of the story. Any suggestion of voter fraud or ballot tampering was considered heresy. It was like they were saying to us Americans, "We have decided the election. Shut up and do as you're told."

The days of trustworthy headlines like the ones below were long gone.

Where was Trump's 37 days? Where was the fairness? Where was the journalistic integrity? Where had all the real reporters gone?

Trump was set up by the Democrats and their paid media thugs. One lies and the others swear by it. That's the way it goes. If you cross their paths, they will take you down. It doesn't matter how big or small you are. Just like Stalin, they will put you in the proverbial gulag and throw away the key. Truth and justice mean nothing to them. It's all about power and control, and they will do anything and say anything to get it.

It doesn't matter who they hurt along the way. Just remember, if they can do it to Trump, they can do it to you—even easier. And as an African American man living in Trenton most of my life, I saw firsthand what it was like to be at their mercy.

CHAPTER 1
EARLY LIFE

Sorry for my lack of manners. Let me make my late mother proud and properly introduce myself. My name is Daryl Mikell Brooks. I was born on September 30, 1968 in Trenton, NJ to Janie Brooks and Robert Griffin. I grew up in Trenton, spent most of my childhood and adult life in Trenton, and when I pass, someone will bring my dead ass back Trenton to be buried. Despite recently moving to Philadelphia, I will always be a Trentonian at heart.

When I grew up, I was what was called a "latch key kid". It was just me and my mother, and she worked full-time at the local condom factory. Because she was always working, I used to have my apartment key on a string, wrapped around my neck. There was no one at home to let me in. I had 5 brothers and sisters on my father's side, but since my parents didn't live together, when I got home from school, it was just me.

You can see my one of my favorite pictures with my mother.

I never met my father or even knew who he was until I was 14. Up until that time, I always thought that my dad was the man my mother was once married to. I used to look through her old wedding album and think that the guy she was with was my father. For years, I went on believing the same thing.

My mother never talked about my father. It was like the man was dead. In fact, I learned who my dad was not from her, but from my favorite aunt. We used to call her affectionately by the name of "sister", and she was my mother's sister-in-law.

My mother was not pleased when "sister" told me my biological father's name or when my uncle introduced me to him. I never knew what happened between the two of them, but I knew it must not have been good for her to never speak of the man.

When I first met my father, he was an OK guy but a little moody at times. I wouldn't say that he neglected me. However, he did leave me standing on the steps of my apartment many times waiting for him, and he never showed up. As a result, he was difficult to understand as a man until my late teen years.

We did have our similarities. We had the same type of hair and the same grin. However, I received my height from my mother's side of the family.

One thing that I really did appreciate was when my dad bought me my first boom box. I used to love playing my tunes on it. However, my mother hated my boom box and tried to throw it out the window at least 3 times. I don't know if she didn't like the music or that I played it too loudly. Maybe, she just wanted to throw it out the window simply because my dad gave it to me. She possibly imagined that she was throwing him out the window and not my prized possession.

About 2 years after my father passed, I was finally introduced to my other half siblings. We have kept in touch ever since that time, and it was a shame that we never met sooner.

When I grew up, I lived in the hood, public housing at its best. Though I grew up poor, I had a working-class mother. She took good care of me. She provided a roof over my head, good food on the table, and clothes to wear. While I was eating steak and fish for dinner, my neighbors in the apartment upstairs were putting hot dogs and pork and beans on the dinner table every night. Unfortunately, that's all they could afford.

At least they had hot dogs. Some people around me had nothing and went hungry. That's a sin. Here in America, people are going hungry. That's just not right. However, I was in the hood, and things like that happened. I was surrounded by poverty. And out of this poverty arises all the drugs, crime and gangs that come with it.

The hood was different back then than it is today. I

remember a bunch of us kids wanted more out of life than to settle for government handouts and an unsafe living environment. Many of us had dreams to do more with our life and not settle for the status quo. In fact, some of the guys I knew eventually made it big after getting a lucrative music contract. They were in a hip-hop group called *Poor Righteous Teachers* and rapped about socially conscious topics. Another one of my friends became a judge, while others went on to successful careers. God bless them. They got out of the hood and did something good with their lives.

Like them, I always felt that the hood was not right for me. I knew better. I'd seen better. My mother's family was originally from St. Mary's, Georgia, and they all did well for themselves. I had an uncle that grew up down there that became a professor at Akron University and had a doctorate in education. Another one of my other uncles that still lived there owned 10 shrimp boats. I'm not saying they were living in a scene from the movie, Forrest Gump, but I am saying that they weren't poor. They all owned their own house, had their own cars, and enjoyed their own private yard. Plus, they didn't have drug addicts running around their neighborhood or the sound of police sirens waking them up at night.

My cousin, Artie "Bubba" Jones, even became the county commissioner of Camden County, Georgia. What a great experience it was when he let me work with him for 10 weeks one summer. I thought I was in heaven. After spending time with him, I was inspired that one day I could run for office and make a change. Hell, if old Bubba could do it, why couldn't I?

Not that I wanted for anything when I was a child, but I used to ask myself all the time, "Why are my cousins, aunts, and uncles living in such a nice place, and I'm in a small apartment in Trenton surrounded by drug addicts?"

Is it wrong to admit that I would have rather lived in Georgia than in the city? I don't think so. Who wouldn't?

Seeing them was my inspiration at a young age. However, most people I knew never saw success, and I believe that if you don't see success, you don't know that you can actually become successful in life.

If you ever go to Trenton, there is this big, lit-up sign on the Lower Trenton Bridge that reads, "TRENTON MAKES. THE WORLD TAKES." What is so ironic about this sign and typifies the entire city is that there is usually a light or two out on one of the letters. Just like the sign, as time went on, the lights in the industrial sector of the city began to go dark as jobs and business moved out, never to be seen again.

After slick Willy, Bill Clinton, sold out the American workers to the NAFTA agreement and the unions became too demanding, all the manufacturing jobs went south, just like the entire Trenton economy. Plus, through poor Democratic leadership, no other significant businesses or industry ever returned. When you go downtown to where all the factories once thrived, there is nothing but rusted out, dilapidated buildings. What once gave the city a chance of becoming a better place had left.

Even as a kid, I tried to do my part to help save the city, and more importantly, the people who lived in it. I knew from a young age that basic building block for success was a good education. Without it, you'd be stuck in public housing all your life. Worse yet, your kids and their kids would be stuck in this same life of poverty. That didn't sit well with me. So when the failing policies of the Trenton Democrats were causing the local North Ward Trenton Library to shut down, I spoke up.

I didn't care that I was just 11. Age didn't mean anything

to me. What meant something was keeping the library open. And as a kid, I knew that the people who it would hurt the most if it closed were the children. Back then, there was no internet or any instant access to information available. The library was all we had. The place was loaded with books, encyclopedias, and magazines. You could spend the whole day there just reading about history, science, and current events. Plus, it was a good escape from the hood. Unlike the violence and poverty on the streets, a library represented a place of learning and, more than that, an opportunity to get ahead.

When the city council was deciding to close the library, I got up and spoke in front of all of them. I pleaded my case. I told them that they couldn't just shut it down. I told them closing the door to the library would be like closing the door to opportunity for the entire black community.

They didn't care what I had to say. The city council shut down the library and locked many of the city kids out of the best chance they had of getting ahead. The worst thing was that none of the Democrats in the city did a damn thing to keep the library open. It just seemed that it wasn't important to them or it didn't matter because it wouldn't further their political careers.

It's like that old African proverb, "It takes a village to raise a child". Unfortunately, the village of Trenton wanted nothing to do with raising any children. It's like they were saying, "They don't vote. So, they don't count." But we did count, and many of my friends and kids that lived in Trenton were left behind as a result.

I was lucky, my mother believed in a good education and made sure I did my homework and studied. But it was my grandmother, Mama Gracie, that instilled in me a strong sense of religion. She was from the south, back in St. Mary's. Going to church and praying every day was instilled in me since a young age. And missing church was not an option. I would get a whooping if I ever tried to skip a service. Sometimes, we even went to 3 different services on a Sunday. If you thought that was a lot, my aunts down in Georgia used to attend church every day.

God became a strong part of my life as a result. And He still is today. Looking back, I can really appreciate that my grandmother instilled good Christian morals in me at such a young age. Hell, I needed them back then and still need them today. Religion is my moral compass that kept me, and still keeps me, from doing anything too stupid at times.

I can't say my entire youth was all that bad. I did have fun and sometime got into a little trouble at times. At age 10, while spending the summer in Georgia, I thought I was a bad-ass and would start my own biker gang. I figured I would be cool going around telling everyone I was a biker kid. It's like somehow that would give me street cred or make me cooler.

So I mustered up a few of my friends and made my "gang". However, we were missing one thing, and that was a motorcycle. People used to tell me, "You can't be in a biker gang if you don't have bikes."

I said that they didn't know what they were talking about. We did have our own bikes. Just because they didn't run on gas or have motors in them didn't mean that they weren't bikes. Our rides ran the old-fashioned way, on sweat and pedals. Yea, we had our own rides. They were called bicycles.

My friends and I got so cocky with our bikes that we rode down to the Camden County Tribune in Saint Mary's and told them about our "gang". They were so impressed that they snapped a picture of us and put it in the paper. The next day when I saw myself featured in print, I thought I was about as bad as they came. I had my own biker gang and article in the Camden County Tribune confirming it.

Looking back, I'm not sure if it were a real slow news day or the reporter thought that we were cute or something. In the end, it didn't matter. That article made me feel like someone important, and to this day, the memory of it still brings a smile to my face.

CHAPTER 2
COLLEGE DAYS

Like I said before, I knew that the best way to get out of the hood was to get a good education. I needed to expand my horizons after graduating Trenton High School and try to accomplish something with my life by attending college.

What interested me the most were people and politics. Though I enjoyed political science, there was no one particular major that I was drawn to. I was in college more just to experience life and to learn from my fellow classmates. While taking these higher education courses, I met people from all different walks of life. There were blacks, whites, and Asians. There were also people from urban and suburban areas, both rich and poor alike. It didn't matter. College was like the great American melting pot where we got to know and learn from one another.

The first stop on my college journey was at Mercer County Community College where I spent 2 years. There, I became the Vice President (VP) of Student Council and was the only African American in the college's student government. And as a freshman, it was a huge accomplishment. Plus, it was the first time I used any political know-how to get the votes I needed for office. I felt like the first slick Willy himself, hobnobbing with different people and shaking various people's hands to get my name out there. However, unlike the politicians in Trenton, I meant what I said and kept my promises. In the end, the students on campus liked me so much that I also became the president of the Black Student Union.

Holding these 2 offices was awesome. Plus, it was a great opportunity to meet more people and get politically involved on campus. I learned more from my fellow students than I did from actually going to class. Getting to know and understand people, all people, was a great opportunity. And only by getting out of the public-school system in Trenton did I have this great chance to broaden my horizons.

After 2 years at Mercer County Community College, I moved onto Camden County College. I took what I learned at Mercer County and started the first black student union there. It was well received by the students and to this day, still exists.

I would have loved to complete my college education at Camden County. However, a lack of funding and an absence of grant money made me take my schooling to the Philadelphia Biblical College, now called Cairn University. Some people may have been discouraged about going from school to school. However, I loved it. The more places I went, the more people I met. No day was a dull one, and everyone I encountered was an opportunity to learn something new.

Plus, I liked the religious aspect to the Philadelphia Biblical College. As I was growing up, God was being pushed more and more out of people's lives and out of the schools. Everything was getting more secular, and religion and God seemed to be getting less and less important. It was amazing how some people I met in college never attended church or even stepped foot in any place of worship. Religion was just not stressed in their houses.

When I think of all of the ways that I have been blessed in my life, it seems like a sin not to go to church or at least say a prayer of thanks to God. If my mother, rest her soul, were still living, she would be saying Amen right now.

Though I knew politics would be in my future, I ended up finishing my schooling at Camden County Tech. There, I graduated with a diploma in the culinary arts.

Good food and good cooking are priceless. And as you can all tell by my physique, I'm not short on either of them.

Plus, I've been able to use these skills throughout my career working as a chef for both high-end and low-end restaurants. Work is work. Whoever wants to pay me to cook, I'll happily bring my spatula.

And no matter where I cooked, the people there were well-fed and coming back for seconds. I've been called a lot of unpleasant things in my life. However, a bad cook was never one of them.

CHAPTER 3
DEMOCRATIC PARTY FAILURE

By going to college and meeting different people from all walks of life, I learned that I, along with all the people in Trenton, were getting played by the Democratic left. I saw what type of students good school systems produced. I learned that the Trenton Democrats were lying to us the entire time and never had our best interest at heart. I realized how towns and small cities could be run so much better, how public schools could be successful, and how businesses could thrive in multiracial communities.

Looking back, I can tell you that the Trenton Democrats failed us since day one. And it all began with their lack of interest in our schools. I already mentioned how they let the local library close without giving it a second thought. Worse yet, they let us go to school without providing any books, or if we did happen to get a book, it was so old that it was falling apart. Hell, how's a kid supposed to learn without schoolbooks?

Plus, there was a lack of school supplies. Most of the students in the Trenton school system were dirt poor. They didn't have money for any school supplies. They were lucky if they even got food on the table at night. As a result, a lot of them didn't have even the basics like paper and pencils. How are you supposed to learn to write without a damn pencil? We couldn't even get a standard number two from our schools. That's not helping any kid. Without proper books, paper, and pencils, school was nothing more than a big babysitting service.

When it came time for answers, the Democrats always blamed the Republicans. Instead of directly confronting the problem, they pointed the finger at the other political party.

"It's their fault," they would tell us.

They would also say that the Republicans were holding up funds and don't care about the black and brown people of America.

In the end, I learned it was one big hoax, a big smoke screen. They had the books, and they had the money. There was no lack of funding by the Republicans. Plus, the Republicans weren't the ones running the government. Democrats held all the positions in the city and much of the state. They were calling the Republicans the boogie men. However, they were the ones calling the shots the entire time. There were no Republicans in office. They had no one to blame but themselves.

The Trenton Times did a story once about the schoolbooks. They reported that the schools had more than enough books. However, for some reason, they were never handed out to the students. They were all locked up in storage, left to rot. Now, how's that supposed to help the kids?

Plus, I want to know why the people who ran the city weren't handing out the books. Did the politicians not want the kids to learn? Did they not want students to achieve? Or simply did the Democratic party want to keep the poor black and brown kids of Trenton uneducated, impoverished, and in constant need of the government's help?

The answer is obvious.

Also, the city of Trenton had plenty of money for the schools. Despite the Democratic finger pointing, they had more than enough funding. The problem was that they squandered much of it. Instead of it going directly to the kids, it went directly to their back pockets.

Money that should have gone to buy paper and pencils was spent on high-paying 6-figure government administration jobs. The worst thing about these jobs is that they weren't even needed. They were nothing more than political payoffs. Instead of hiring a bunch of overpaid pencil-pushers, the Democrats should have done what was right and bought some proper school supplies for the kids.

So what type of students do you think Trenton public schools produced in the end? Instead of turning out literate kids who could make something of their lives, they churned out many students who were functionally illiterate. How that hell can you get a good job if you can't even read? You can't. You'd be lucky to get a simple service job flipping burgers at McDonalds. That's all you're trained to do.

The poor education ultimately led to increased school dropout and increased illiteracy rates in inner-city communities. Without a proper education or a chance of getting a well-paying job, it led to increased crime, the rise of gangs, and increased use of drugs. Without proper training, these kids in Trenton were destined for a life of poverty and failure.

Plus, poverty would perpetuate poverty and a lack of education would perpetuate a lack of education. It became a generational problem. The entire family became stuck in this whole vicious cycle. Worse yet, it became the societal norm. Being poor and functionally illiterate somehow became acceptable.

Instead of the schools pumping out kids that would become doctors, lawyers, or engineers, they were pumping out untrained and unqualified workers without much hope for their future.

Plus, many of the students who did go to college were completely unprepared because they never properly learned the basics. In the end, many were forced to drop out because they simply couldn't keep up. How's a kid supposed to excel in higher learning when they never received the basic building blocks of a good education?

Some of the answers of how to fix this mess were straight forward. However, the Trenton politicians never had any interest in doing anything about it. If you want to help these kids from a young age, begin their education early on. Start at age 3 with quality pre-kindergarten classes. The data is irrefutable. The best long-term predictor of student achievement is the quality of education he or she receives from birth to age 5. That is the time of maximum brain development. Plus, public education needs to be more than just about teaching kids the 3R's (reading, writing and arithmetic). Schools also need to teach kids about how to become good people. Because many were not receiving such basic information at home or on the streets, the school system must fill in these necessary gaps.

In addition, instead of hiring more high-paid, pencil pushing administrators, hire more teachers. And send the teachers that were already there to courses in order to sharpen their skills.

Another thing that really turned me off about the Democrats was that Crime Bill signed by our so-called, beloved president, Slick Willy Clinton. That sly politician said it would help inner-city city kids, but instead, it made the poor black and brown communities worse off than they were already.

Plus, don't forget the congressman who sponsored this bill. Yea, it was that plagiarizing swamp-creature himself, Joe Biden. I remember that hyena sitting behind Clinton in the south lawn of the White House as he signed the bill into law. Grinning from side to side, Biden didn't give a damn about the people of color in the city. He just wanted them locked up and taken off the streets. The mainstream media never covered that story in the 2020 presidential election.

The crime bill was a disaster since the day it passed. It was obvious, and all of us living in the hood knew it. However, the Trenton Democrats embraced it as if the bill were the best thing ever to come out of Washington, DC. Hell, they were like mindless sheep being brought to slaughter. Just because Clinton said it would be good, they followed along without a peep of dissent.

If you don't know what the Crime bill is, let me explain it to you. First of all, that's not its real name. It's called the Violent Crime Control and Law Enforcement Act. The law was passed in an effort by the Democrats, including Clinton and Biden, to "get tough on crime".

It had parts in it like the "three strike provision" whereby repeat criminal offenders were given life sentences and taken off the streets and out of the free society for good. Plus, it got rid of any chance of rehabilitation for the growing prison population by taking away the higher education grant. Instead of attempting to give prisoners a chance to make something better of their lives when they get out of jail through some sort of education, they were worse off than when they were first incarcerated.

The Crime Bill also created new laws that mandated jail time if broken and authorized stiffer criminal penalties.

One example was how people were getting a mandatory extra 10 years added to their sentence if they committed a crime within a thousand feet of a school. Hell, the schools were placed right in the center of the city where everyone lived. It was bad enough getting locked up for selling a little pot. Now, people were sent to the slammer for at least 10 years.

In the end, this bill ultimately decimated the inner-city population. It took fathers out of homes, destroyed families, and created even more poverty. Instead of preventing crime, the poverty, lack of education, and lack of rehabilitation for the inmates led to increased crime and more social and economic problems for the inner-city population.

It also created a massive incarceration boom. According to the Department of Justice, under Bill Clinton and Joe Biden, the U.S. prison population swelled to nearly 2 million people, with blacks as the main victims. The incarceration for blacks increased from about 3,000 per 100,000 to 3,620 per 100,000 at this time.

The Trenton Democrats bought into programs like the Crime Bill and told us they would be best for our communities. Despite laws like the Crime Bill proving to be a colossal failure, they continued to endorse it.

You know what I call politicians like this?

"Poverty pimps."

They don't care about the people. They just wanted to pimp them out for their votes. Every time an election would come around, they would go door to door, shaking hands and smiling at the people. With their fake grins, they would promise to do something about the poverty, create jobs, end gangs, and bring prosperity back to Trenton.

The politicians would also try to buy our votes by handing out free food like chicken dinners or hot dogs.

Gimmicks like this would unfortunately always work. And the people of Trenton would believe their false promises and lies, year after year.

I remember hearing my neighbors shouting out to them, "We'll vote for you. We'll vote for you!"

Then, when the election was over, there wasn't a politician in sight. One minute they acted as if they were our best friend. The next, they were nowhere in sight. Hell, a person would have a better chance of spotting big foot or the loch ness monster than they would of seeing a politician in an off-election year.

The joke was that the Trenton politicians said that they were there to fix the problem. The truth was that they were the problem. Democrats controlled the entire government and every aspect of it. From top to bottom, it was completely run by Democrats. Instead of making things better when they were in power, they made it worse.

Plus, they kept getting elected. No matter how much the crime increased, the inner-city city problems worsened, or the poverty became, they got back into office, year after year.

Albert Einstein once said, "The definition of insanity is doing the same thing over and over again but expecting different results."

And that's what it was—insane. I couldn't help but ask myself how these people who are destroying the city kept getting back into office. It was a damn shame, but that's what was happening in the inner-city.

Insanity.

What it created was an entire population of people on welfare. Generation after generation, entire families became tied to the government dole. Instead of working and providing food and shelter for themselves, they were forced to hold out their hand and beg for the crumbs that the government would give them.

Welfare became the new norm. Somehow, not working and waiting for a monthly welfare check became acceptable. It was no longer looked down upon that you weren't working or trying to get ahead. Instead, it seemed almost expected.

Plus, the politicians would promote these welfare programs. They would tell us the more kids we had, the more money the government would give us. They would also show us what we had to do to get all the government freebies that we were "owed".

Hell, what they should have been doing is showing us a path to get off the government dole and be able to support our damn lives. Instead of promoting poverty, they should have been promoting education or some sort of specialized training.

The truth is that it's all about being dependent on them. I don't think that they ever wanted us to think for ourselves or get a proper education. I believe that's why they never gave the inner-city kids any new books or supplies. A proper education from day one would have taught the kids that to get ahead you have to depend on yourself and not on the government.

The politicians wanted to lead us around like a bunch of mindless sheep, telling us what to do with our lives, how to live our lives, and how to vote. And dammit if most of us never knew any better.

I guess that's why some of the city folk kept on voting for them. They were afraid that if they didn't put those same politicians back in power, they would no longer get their welfare check and other government handouts. It's like that old saying, "Don't bite the hand that feeds you."

Many of the underprivileged people knew that without their monthly government check, they would have nothing. There would be no money for food, no money for entertainment, and no money to do anything. And without the most basic of education, what are you gonna do? What can you do?

Nothing.

And that's how these poverty pimps remained in power and are still there now. Trenton is worse off than it ever was. Plus, there is no damn end in sight to this downward spiral.

Sometimes I go down the streets and just lament about how bad the city has become. It looks like a war zone you would see on one of those History Channel documentaries. I just think of all those businesses and jobs that were lost. Worse yet, I think of all the lives that were destroyed as a result of the poverty and crime.

One other thing that I think added to the decline of the inner-city were those violent video games. You may think, "What's a video game got to do with this? It's just a game. There's no harm in it."

However, these games aren't like the Pacman and Donkey Kong of my day. No, these games are now full of killing, raping, and robbing. I'm not sure if you ever heard of Grand Theft Auto or Call of Duty. Well, if you didn't, let me tell you a little bit about them. They are nothing but violence. Pimping hoes, stealing cars, running over people, and murdering sums up the objectives of most of them.

What type of example is that for a young kid? Plus, these kids start off playing them when they are less than 8 years of age. How's a kid supposed to act normal if he spends most of the day in his bedroom exposed to and participating in violence? If a person sees constant violence, he or she is most likely to act violent. They get numb to the death, murder, and destruction by constantly playing these games.

According to Albert Bandura, Jordan Professor of Social Sciences in Psychology at Stanford University, "Later research has shown that viewing violent acts on TV and in the movies affects people in other negative ways." He believed that it decreased viewers' concern about victims' suffering and decreased their sensitivity to violent acts. Watching violence also increased the likeliness that a person would copy the aggressive acts they were witnessing. He went on to add that younger children were the most susceptible.

I saw that issue play out exactly in my own high school. Just like on video games and in the movies, the school was full of violence. The vice-principal of the school was once quoted as saying, "I see the way our students communicate on a daily basis. They don't have enough opportunities to practice appropriate communication with each other that doesn't involve violence and suspicion."

Just like that dude Devin Moore who gunned down those cops in Alabama in 2003. His lawyer blamed his killing spree on, among other things, violent video games. Supposedly, he spent most of his day playing Grand Theft Auto: Vice City. And after he was finally arrested, Devin said, "Life is a video game. You've gotta die sometime."

Yea, we all gotta die, but hopefully it's at an old age surrounded by loved ones and not due to a violence-filled crime spree or killing rampage.

Devon was just a kid and look at what horrible things he did with his life. I know a lot of the so-called experts say it's a bunch of nonsense, believing video games cause violence. However, I say that's a bunch of crap. Of course, if you see violence on the TV all day, it will definitely make you more inclined to act it out. The shock value in committing a crime or a killing is essentially gone if you did it virtually on a video game day after day for thousands of times.

Devin Moore is not alone. There's Adam Lanza from the Sandy Hook murders, Kimveer Gill Dawson of the College shootings, and Eric Harris and Dylan Klebold of the Columbine massacre.

What's one thing all these kids had in common?

They were all addicted to violent video games.

Many of these young kids like Devon never had a positive role model in the household or were left alone all day with nothing to do. Instead of having someone there to properly raise them, video games and other violence they saw on TV became some sort of surrogate parent.

If these inner-cities were run properly, kids would have better things to do with their lives instead of wasting it on these damn games. They would have homework to finish, books to read, safe places to play, or jobs where they can work. However, the city offered none of that.

So when people ask me why I left the Democratic party, it's a simple answer. I didn't leave them. They left me and all the other black, brown, and poor people of the inner-city.

CHAPTER 4
DOUBLE-CROSS

Just like many of my friends back in the day, the hood eventually caught up to me. Sometimes, no matter what you are doing or how well you are doing it, the past has a way of creeping up on you and biting you right when you don't expect it. Worse yet, sometimes the ones doing the biting are that exact people you are trying to help.

It happened on April 19, 1995, the day of the Oklahoma City Bombing. Just like most people that day, I could not stop thinking about this horrific domestic act of terrorism. The picture of half of the Alfred P. Murrah Federal Building blown up was just awful. Plus, the needless loss of life, especially of the children in the nursery, made me sick.

In order to get this picture out of my mind, I wanted to do something positive—something that would make a meaningful difference in people's lives. Back in the day, I had this friend named Dexter Smith. He was a former drug addict that turned his life around and now was spending time with kids trying to get them off drugs.

In 1995, crack was hot. It filled our streets and was a real problem. Guys would get addicted to that stuff, and it would ruin their entire lives. Worse yet, it would ruin the lives of everyone around them, including loved ones and family. For some, it was an absolute death sentence.

That day, I went with Dexter to the Trenton Rehabilitation Center, just as we did many times. We would spend time there talking to the troubled people that entered the doors. Dexter and I did our best to counsel them and be there for them during their time of need. My friend would try to inspire everyone with his life's story. He would explain about his own drug problem, and how he fought through the addiction to go on and have a normal, productive life. No matter how many times he told it, I could not hear it enough. Plus, we were getting through to some of these kids.

It was amazing. It's like no one ever told them that there was more in life than doing drugs, selling drugs, or living on the street. Many of these people never had words of inspiration or hope ever spoken to them. It's sad. Imagine never getting a pat on the back or having someone telling you that your life mattered or that you were important. No wonder why many of them never got off the drugs; they felt like there was nothing for them in the end, even if they beat the habit.

After spending my afternoon at the rehabilitation center, I walked through Martin Luther King, Jr. Park and stopped to talk to a friend who was a baseball coach and a preacher. I knew the guy for years and he could talk all day to a person without a problem.

However, I had to go home, change my clothes, and pick up my bible. I didn't want to be late for my young ministers training at Galilee Baptist Church. Plus, I felt like that day was a day when I really needed to pray, especially after the seeing what happened in Oklahoma. Who better else to talk to than God during times of trouble?

I remember coming back home after the training, and my mom telling me that the cops were looking for me.

Why were the cops looking for me? It made no sense.

So, instead of waiting for them to come back, I called up the police station myself and asked what the problem was. I knew I hadn't stolen anything or committed a crime. That's just not me.

Two cops then came right over to the house. One was name Earl Hill. He was a big ass dude with red hair and stood at 6 foot seven inches. His nickname was "Big Red", and he was known as one nasty police officer. In fact, he was on trial already for unjustly beating someone up while on duty. The other cop was some white guy named Leon Letts. No one had any beef with him, and, unlike his partner, he had a good reputation around town.

I welcomed both officers into the house, even "Big Red". They then told me that there was a report of me flashing some kids while drinking a bottle of brandy. I told them the only thing that I was flashing that day was the Bible, and they were looking for the wrong person.

They cops then informed me that they wanted to take me to the scene of the supposed crime so that they could see if these kids could ID me. Wanting to prove my innocence, I had no problem going with them. I wanted this whole thing to be over, and I thought that if I quickly cleared my name, it would be the end of this problem.

When we arrived at the alleged scene of the crime, the cops knocked on the door. There was no one home except for 2 little girls ages 11 and 9 who answered the door. The cops then went into the house, and I stayed outside, waiting for them.

After standing out there for what seemed like hours, the cops came back to the front door and asked the girls if I was the man who flashed them.

Though I had seen neither of them before, one of them pointed directly at me and shook her head. I was shocked.

No damn way!

The whole story didn't make sense.

To begin with, where were these kid's parents?

The cops then went on to tell me that the girls alleged that I exposed myself in front of pole outside their house, next to a police mini-station.

I looked at them as if to say, "You expect me to believe that I would be dumb enough to commit such a crime, and do it, right in front of a bunch of cops?"

Plus, the crime supposedly took place in broad daylight, in the middle of a bustling North Trenton public housing project in Donnelly Homes, and the only witnesses were these 2 girls. I'm a 6 foot five, tall black man. It's not like I don't stand out in a crowd, especially if I were standing there naked from the waist down.

What didn't make sense either was that these girls said I was drinking brandy. I asked myself that if I had a bottle in my hand, how could they identify it as alcohol at that distance? Plus, how could they be so sure it was a bottle of brandy? They were kids.

In addition, if I were drinking that day and intoxicated, I should have at least received a breathalyzer test to corroborate the story. I didn't even get one of those by the cops.

No. Something was not right with this whole story, and I knew I was innocent.

After leaving the girls' home, the cops let me go. There were no charges, and I was not brought back to the police station. At that time, I honestly thought this whole thing was over. I mean, how could I be arrested for anything? First of all, I didn't do it. And second of all, the entire case was based upon the testimony of 2 kids that I never seen before, who were left home alone.

That night I went home and gave it no more thought, believing the whole thing was behind me. There was no case.

It all made sense a little later when I found out who these 2 girls were. These were no random kids sitting innocently in their house, looking out the window. No, they were the daughters of a prominent drug dealer, to whom I had been having "words" with recently.

That truth was that the dad didn't like the anti-drug message I was preaching around town. Why would he? Trenton was full of loyal customers who came back day after day for their hit. My message of a better future and of a life without drugs cut directly into his sick business model.

And the man was not subtle in letting me know how he felt. On one occasion, a week prior to the accusation, he and 2 of his brothers jumped me in the street in order to teach me a lesson. They thought that by ruffing me up, I would run scared.

I wasn't afraid of a little beating. In fact, I continued to preach my message despite the assault. These thugs didn't scare me.

In fact, the people who ran the whole damn city didn't scare me. I needed to speak my mind. Our city and people inside of it were dying, and no one was doing anything to help. Someone needed to be the voice of reason. Someone needed to speak for those that couldn't or were too afraid to speak for themselves. And that was me.

My heroes and inspiration have always been Dr. Martin Luther King, Jr. and Malcolm X. I wanted to be just like them, fighting for the underprivileged and preaching against those trying to keep us black folks down. It was the right thing to do. Their success inspired me to do the same.

I took my message all the way to the top. In fact, I spoke out about the mayor at that time, Doug Palmer, for his incompetence in dealing with the real problems that faced Trenton. I also had words with our local Westward Councilman, Bill Young, about his ineffectiveness as a leader. Plus, I didn't score any points with cops as I spoke out about police brutality and racial profiling.

I was just trying to help the black and underprivileged community in our city. If it meant ruffling a few feathers, I would have no problem doing it.

Unfortunately, my message was not accepted by those in charge. In fact, they saw me as some sort of instigator or threat and wanted to shut me up. I think the final straw occurred 13 days after my initial incident with the police. After a heated verbal discussion with Councilman Young, he ended the conversation by telling me that the police had been looking for me and needed to see me down at the station.

It was a threat, and I knew it. However, I wasn't going to play that game. Naïve me at the time told him I'd be happy to go down to the police station since I had nothing to hide. In the heat of the moment, I thought nothing about the conversation or how convenient it was for him to tell me that the police were looking for me after the argument.

If the cops were really looking for me, why hadn't one of them come to my house for the last 13 days? They knew where I lived. They at least could have called or stopped by to speak with my mother. And why, only after this one particular argument, did Young mention the cops were looking for me? He could have informed me earlier in the week when I saw him or maybe at the beginning of the conversation.

No. This whole thing was a set up. Did Bill Young call

the police after I left and tell them that I was coming down to the station? I don't know. But what I do know, looking back, is that my mother raised no fool. This whole thing was more than just a coincidence.

It looked like I finally upset the wrong person.

After calling the police to let them know I was coming to the station, I was met by Detective Buddy Law when I got there—alone. I had no lawyer. There was no one there to represent me, and no rights were ever given to me.

After giving Buddy Law my deposition, I was photographed, and my ass was eventually put into a photo police lineup. The whole time I was asking myself, "What the hell is going on? I'm innocent."

After the 2 kids who I allegedly flashed from a distance, in the middle of broad daylight, in front of a police mini-station pointed me out, I was taken into custody and charged with 2 counts of sexual assault, 2 counts of endangerment of a child, and 2 counts of lewdness—one count for each of the kids.

Wow!

To make matters worse, the next day Joe Constance, the former police director, gave an impassioned statement to the news media that people like me needed to be locked up.

How could he say this? There was no investigation, and the case was still far from going to court. Yet, he proclaimed my guilt in front of everyone. Due process be damned and the thought of being innocent until proven guilty never crossed his mind.

In the press conference, Joe Constance went as far as to tell the reporters that I would break into houses and steal women's underwear, and it was only a matter of time before I went on to commit more crimes.

There was absolutely no reason or basis for him to

make such absurd statements. I had no previous arrests and had never gave the police any trouble.

Where was my due process? It reminded me of the 4 days it took the press to declare Biden the winner after the 2020 election. Just like in my circumstance, Trump's legal case had not even gone to court. However, they were already declaring him the loser.

Where were our 37 days?

It's like the decision was already made. End of story.

At least Gore was given the chance in the media's eye to show his side of the story.

There was no mercy. The hit was out. If I were just charged with flashing (as mandated correctly by the law), the case would have just stayed in municipal court. However, with those 6 charges, the trial needed to go to superior court. And that court meant stiffer penalties and longer incarceration if I were found guilty.

They were throwing the book at me. Drug dealers and criminals got off easier.

Luckily, friends and family helped me post the $10,000 bail, and I got the hell out of jail.

I felt betrayed and disillusioned.

My own people turned against me. While growing up, I always thought it was us black folk and underprivileged against the world, fighting for what is right. I knew we wouldn't always agree with each other, but I never even considered the possibility that they would turn against me. I thought the great struggle was black against white, not black verses black. However, that was what it came down to.

It just didn't make sense. My mind was blown.

For days, I was in a state of shock. I could simply not get over the fact that my own people betrayed me. I was framed, lied about, and blackballed by my fellow black man.

I needed to get out of Trenton. After making sure it was legal, I left the city with the little pride I still had and relocated to Camden. It was time to move on with my life and pray for the best.

Thank God for my faith in the Lord. He got me through these hard times. Without him, I know I would have gone crazy, or did possibly something that I would have regretted.

After finally coming to terms with the charges, I felt confident the legal system would vindicate me. I've watched those cop shows on TV and thought I knew how the whole process worked. On these programs, the cops and investigators would canvass the crime scene, bring in evidence, and get statements from witnesses. They would then bring it all together in order to see if there really were a justifiable case and if the accused person actually committed the crime.

In fact, I was so confident the investigation would vindicate me, I took a while to find a lawyer. "Why not?" I thought. I'm innocent. When the cops investigate the evidence, they will discover that there was no case against me.

Eventually, I did get a lawyer that I trusted and one who believed in me. His name was Jack Ceelig. We got along great, and he understood the exact circumstances surrounding the case.

Jack was once quoted as saying, "Daryl is one of those cases where I knew he was completely innocent."

With him on my side, I went on with my life and tried my best not to think about the impending case. It's not like the legal system was in any rush. In fact, it took another three and a half years before I saw my first day in court.

You would have thought I'd be nervous. However, I was looking forward to it. I believed the whole thing was in the bag. Plus, my reputation needed to be cleared, and I wanted this whole damn charade to be behind me.

As the trial unfolded, it went exactly as I expected. The prosecution had no evidence against me. Other than the 2 girls, there were no other witnesses, photos, or proof of my guilt. The case entirely rested on the children.

Plus, Reverend Harris of Galilee Baptist Church testified that I was at the young ministers training class when the alleged crime supposedly took place.

What was crazy about the trial, though, was when they brought the oldest daughter up to the stand and asked her who was the flasher. She couldn't even point me out. Her mother needed to point directly in my direction so she could "identify" me.

That's not right. In fact, one of the alternative jurors, Gilbert Bell, came to my mother's house after the trial and told her exactly what he saw. He was so distraught about my case that he took it upon himself to speak with her.

Unfortunately, no one else seemed to catch the mother's prompting.

Even if the prosecution did, the whole case was nothing more than just one big hit. The politicians and drug dealers who I had been speaking out against wanted me out of the way. And if meant using these kids, that's what they would do.

What was even more disappointing about the trial was that I learned the cops never really did a proper investigation. They never canvassed the alleged crime scene or searched for witnesses who would either clear my name or corroborate the prosecution's story.

Throughout the trial, it felt like I had to prove my innocence instead of the legal system proving my guilt.

Because the prosecution had little evidence to support their case, it came down to how much could I prove that I was innocent.

That's not how the law should work.

Plus, I always thought that the jury should consist of your own peers. Unfortunately, it wasn't. There were no other black men on the entire jury except Gilbert Bell, and he was just a designated alternate, which meant that he had no vote.

Because of the lack of evidence, I thought the jurors would eventually find me innocent of all 6 charges. In fact, when I rose to hear the verdict, the first 2 counts came back not guilty. What a relief! If I were found innocent against one of the girls, then I would definitely be found innocent for the other who was allegedly standing next to her.

However, the other 4 counts came out guilty. Each count of guilt was like a jagged dagger being stuck in my back. As they read them one by one, it was as if they were saying instead: betrayed by his own people, turned on by the legal system, forgotten by the police, and not important.

Stab, stab, stab, and stab.

The people who were out to get me were not only hurting me, but they were hurting my entire family. I already had one kid and another on the way. Now, they both would have to be raised without a father. Plus, I thought my poor mother was going to die of a heart attack right there in the courtroom. Imagine the stress the verdict put on her.

I'm also disappointed with the jury. It's not like there was a clear case against me or any definitive evidence. If there were, the verdict would have come immediately. Instead, it took 2 whole weeks for them to decide.

Gilbert Bell also told my mother, "(There) was too many conflicting stories between the police". He also said, "Some people had their mind made up before they came into the courtroom (that Daryl was guilty)."

What was most telling was that Gilbert also recalled that were at least three jurors who thought I was innocent. When he approached one of them on why they'd changed their vote, the juror replied, "Everyone else said he was guilty. So I went along with it."

Does this sound "beyond reasonable doubt"?

After the verdict was read, I was surrounded by 10 armed guards. What did they think I was going to do? Run? I had no history of violence, drugs, or previous run-ins with the police before. They were like a pack of wolves ready to descend on their prey.

Of course, I let them put on the handcuffs. What choice did I have?

The travesty of this whole situation didn't end with the verdict. In the sentencing part of the case, the prosecution asked for 15 damn years. Murderers, drug dealers, and real sex offenders got less time than that! Plus, I had no previous criminal record and was not any type of repeat offender.

It was the lowest point in my life. I felt dejected and disenfranchised. All I could think about was what went wrong or what could I have done differently.

The thought of never being able to go home ever again ran through my mind over and over again. It was like a bad song that could not get out of my head. All I could visualize was the end of my freedom and never being able to do what I wanted to do or go where I wanted to go ever again.

I would have felt better if the cops would have put the handcuffs around my neck instead of my wrists. At least it would have relieved my utter sadness.

The words of Dr. King brought me solace in my greatest time of need. Instead of perseverating on my circumstances, I thought of one of his many sermons:

Don't ever think you're by yourself. Go on to jail if necessary, but you'll never go alone. Take a stand for that which is right, and the world may misunderstand you and criticize you, but you never go alone. For somewhere I read that "one with God is a majority," and God has a way of transforming a minority into a majority. Walk with Him this morning and believe in Him and do what is right and He'll be with you even until the consummation of the ages.

In the end, the court gave me 7 years flat and hauled me off to jail.

Despite the loss, I never blamed my lawyer. He did the best he could. However, when the cards are stacked against you, winning sometimes is not an option. It's like the ballot boxes were stuffed in favor of the prosecution, and no matter how much evidence of my innocence that I showed, the prosecution would manufacture more ballots to put me away.

That's where they wanted to keep me. In fact, when I initially went to jail, the same prosecution team that locked me up tried to get me to stand in a police lineup. They said that they needed tall, black men to stand side by side so that the witness could identify the perpetrator.

I was promised some donuts for my help.

Do I look like I need donuts?

What did these clowns think I was going to do, sell my soul for some Dunkin' Donuts?

What happened if this witness went on to pick me out of this lineup as the criminal? I was already falsely accused. Why the hell now would I want to tempt fate?

As I said before, my mother didn't raise a fool. I told the prosecutors "Hell no," and that they could take those donuts and shove them where the sun doesn't shine.

CHAPTER 5
INJUSTICE SERVED

After the sentencing, I initially went to the Mercer County Correctional facility to be held over until I went to prison. It was utterly embarrassing.

When I lived in Trenton, I knew everybody. It was like I was the de facto mayor of the city, even though I never took office.

That was great when I was a free man. However, now in jail, I knew many of the guards and prisoners. Some were old friends. Others, I went to school with or at least knew one of their siblings.

All the guys I met there were shocked, and more importantly, disappointed to see me. Many of them looked up to me as a community leader and as someone who was going to make a difference in the city. Now, here in prison, I was just another thug with little chance of redemption.

I felt like I let them down. I felt like I let myself down.

Don't get me wrong, I was treated well. However, I could see the disappointment in their eyes. Though no one said anything, I could feel it.

Thank God for my mother. She was my guardian angel and saving grace. That saint of a woman stayed by my side the entire time. While I was in holding, she found an appeals lawyer named Leroy Carmichael who promised to get me out of jail in 3-4 months.

Unfortunately, the man was a snake oil salesman and had no experience in dealing with cases such as mine. The man's clientele were mostly drug dealers and common thugs. My circumstances were different. Instead of helping me out, he squandered the money I gave my mother.

In fact, during the appeal, the judge threw the case out of court because he failed to file the proper documentation. Instead of correcting his error, Leroy kept the money that we paid him and never returned.

And that was my first and last appeal. Without any money, I was now at the mercy of the prison system.

After holding, I was sent to Southern State Correctional Facility. What shocked me initially about this place was that everyone there was walking around in regular street clothes. People had on jeans and jewelry and were playing their radios. I expected everyone to be wearing uniforms and be locked up in cells.

The place looked like some sort of summer camp. However, it was prison, and you couldn't leave and were surrounded by correction officers, or CO's as we called them, who all had guns. Instead of cells, there were trailers where the prisoners slept with courtyards and basketball courts in between them.

It all seemed weird to me, and it was difficult to acclimate myself to this type of living. As an only child, I had my own bedroom and my own privacy. I never said I was some sort of prima donna. However, I do like a little privacy. Living in this dorm-like facility felt uncomfortable.

When I went to bed, there were a bunch of dudes lying next to me and above me.

I would have rather been placed in a small cell all by myself than be in the trailer, full of other people. Despite the open spaces, the entire place felt claustrophobic.

Plus, as a black activist fighting for the people all my life, I was shocked to see how I was treated. Despite Dr. Martin Luther King, Jr's incarceration and beating, the man was considered a hero. He was my hero. I looked up to guys like that who were willing to speak their mind and fight for what's right.

I thought the black community in the prison would give me at least some of the same respect. I was on their side, fighting against poverty, drugs, violence, and police brutality. I stood toe to toe with the mayor, police chief, and all the drug dealers around the city of Trenton, preaching my word of peace, equality, and education.

Instead, these guys turned their backs on me. Both the CO's and prisoners would call me a rapist or a child molester, among other things.

Jesus said, "Let him who is without sin cast the first stone." And it's not like these guys had no faults. They weren't sentenced to go to prison because they were reading the Bible too long during the day or helped out too many days at the soup kitchen. No, they were sent there for admittedly committing a crime. It's not like any of the guys I met there denied what they did.

Again, I felt as if my own people let me down. The romantic struggle of black versus white, us versus them, was just an illusion. It wasn't the white people who were out to get me, it was the other black folk who put me here in prison and who were now mocking me everywhere that I went.

One main thing I learned with this whole experience

was that white people were not the problem. It was our own damn people now turning on each other that was causing most of the difficulties. It was black on black crime that was an issue.

It was a crime how the black politicians were running the city. It was a crime how blacks were selling drugs to other blacks and destroying their lives in the process.

Hell. We should be working together. This was not what Dr. King intended.

One thing I learned in life is that you are who you respond to. When the prisoners and CO's called me a rapist or horrible names, I wouldn't respond to them. That's not who I was, nor who I would become. I am an honest, God-fearing man who wants to make myself a better person and make the lives of everyone I meet better in the process.

While in prison, I was able to get at least a little street cred. Being 6 foot five with a good vertical leap made me a favorite on the basketball court. Back in the day, I had some good moves and one hell of a jump shot. In fact, the prisoners and CO's would put money on me to win the games.

Some guys before the match would come up to me and ask how many rebounds do I think I would have or how many baskets do I think that I would make. Depending on what I told them or how I felt, they would make a larger bet.

Basketball was a way out for me. It let me take my mind off the circumstances and my unjust imprisonment. Plus, when I pulled off a big win, I'd find all sorts of "presents" in my bed. I got such prizes as canned food and packs of cigarettes. It was like Christmas to see what all was on my blanket. I never smoked, but I did appreciate the gratitude people showed me.

One other good thing about this prison was that

food could be brought in from the outside. My mother would bring me in my favorite shrimp dish whenever she had a chance. Plus, the food inside the correction facility wasn't that bad. It's not like what you think you would get in a prison. There was fried chicken, mashed potatoes, and other good desserts. That stuff could really fatten a guy up after a while.

Just when I started feeling comfortable in the prison, I came to the realization of "What the hell am I doing here?" I never wanted to get acclimated to prison life or accommodate to this false incarceration. I didn't belong in this place and never wanted to feel that way.

I was an innocent man being unjustly locked up. As days went on, anger built up inside me. I was missing my family, my friends, and my home. The prison was not my home and the inmates were not my real friends.

The one-year mark was my breaking point. I had enough. After one of the other prisoners got cocky with me, I responded this time with my fists instead of turning my back. A man can only take so much.

Not surprisingly, the correctional facility did not look too kindly on violence. As punishment, I was sent to Trenton State Prison Ad Seg, which was solitary confinement. Ironically, I was in the same wing that Rubin "Hurricane" Carter was incarcerated when he was in prison.

If you don't know, "Hurricane" Carter was a famous boxer who was wrongfully locked up for 20 years after being convicted of a murder that he never committed. His story actually became a movie, and the lead role was played by Denzel Washington.

Not that I was in his same cell, but I did think about him while I was in that prison. I could not help but draw similarities between his innocence and mine.

I know Ad Seg had a bad reputation. However, it did offer one positive thing. I got to sleep alone. It was the first good night sleep I had in over a year. Though I considered myself a people-person, I like a little space to myself at night, even if it meant solitary confinement.

I spent a total of 6 months in all doing solitary, 3 months at Ad Seg and another 3 at Rahway State Prison, now known as East Jersey State Prison. Regardless of where they put me, it was still prison, and I was away from my family, friends, and other loved ones.

What hurt while I was there was the fact that not a single person from my own place of worship, Shiloh Baptist Church, ever came to see me. They were supposed to be Christian folk, there to support other Christians in their time of need. Well, being unjustly locked up away from my mom and kids was my time of need.

I was also aggravated with the people of Trenton and the black community as a whole. Here I was, the guy standing up for their rights and advocating for a better place to live, and not a single person seemed to care about my unjust incarceration.

Hell, if the tables were turned and one of the activists that I worked with got unfairly locked up, I would have had marches, created a mass telephone campaign, and had people call the local politicians, the mayor, the senator, and even governor.

However, I went away without a peep.

Forgotten. Good riddance.

Times like these make you fall to your knees and question everything and everyone. You ask yourself, "Why me?" and, "Why did God let this happen?"

It makes even a religious man question the entire so-called Christian community and his own faith in God.

It reminded me of a story in the Old Testament

when Joseph, son of Isaac, was sold into slavery by his brothers and then locked up in jail after being unjustly accused of sexual assault. Just like my story, Joseph never committed the crime, and the accusation was maliciously put forward as a means of retaliation and retribution.

Maybe God planned out this whole ordeal for me, just like he did for Joseph. In the end of the biblical story, Joseph was vindicated and eventually became the Vizier of Egypt, second in command only to the pharaoh himself. Maybe God has something great for me in the future. Maybe this entire ordeal was meant to teach me something or take me somewhere in life that I couldn't go without having spent time in jail.

One man, in particular, helped me to maintain my Christian faith after being rejected by my own church and religious community. He was a white preacher from the southern bible conference who visited the prison and spoke with us inmates. What was different about him was that he really understood what was happening behind bars and cared for the prisoners.

He used to preach to us how prisons were innately evil institutions that needed reform. He would speak about how prisoners were worse off after they were incarcerated than they were before ever being locked up, and the only thing the prison system produced was life-long prisoners. He used to say how the men and women released from jail were full of hate and violence and were trained to do nothing else but go back to a life of crime.

What was even more inspirational about the man was that he was the only clergyman who would bring a letter I wrote to the newspapers outside of prison for me. Even the black Baptist ministers and the Imams who visited the jail refused to do this one little thing for me. I will never forget the man, nor will I ever stop praying for him. He was like an angel sent to the prison to help me maintain my faith in God and in humanity.

After 6 months in the hole, I was transferred to Riverfront State Prison in Camden. This location was great for my mother. Because it was an easy ride from Trenton, she would frequently visit me and bring my 2 kids. I'd look forward to those days all week, and it helped the time fly by quicker while in prison.

However, Riverfront proved no different than Southern State. The dudes there were just as cruel. I'd come back to my bed at night and find out some guy pissed in it or threw their drink on it. Foul language, accusations, and sneers followed me everywhere I went. They all thought I was some sort of child molester and treated me as such much of the time I was there. Thank God I'm 6 foot five and am good with my fists. I can just imagine what would have happened if the guys thought that they could physically abuse me.

One thing I did learn in prison was how to think for other people. Another way of saying it is that I learned to understand what the other guy was thinking and not just react to how they were acting. Remember, many of these guys in prison don't know anything but violence and brutality. If you simply react to their violent attitude, the situation will always turn out negatively. However, if you understand their frame of mind, you learn how to avoid conflict and potentially make friends. It's a life skill that cannot be taught. It's one that you must learn.

After over 3 years in prison, thank God my first parole hearing finally arrived. I knew that I had to make this day count and do everything I could to get the hell out of jail. In fact, while in prison, I did my best to take these so-called courses they taught on non-violence, rehab, and even cooking. I would have taken a course on fingerpainting if it meant I could leave jail earlier. However, the one thing I would not do for parole was admit that I was guilty. In fact, some of the other prisons tried to coach me on how to make sure I got paroled. They would all advise me to tell the parole board exactly what they wanted to hear, even if it meant admitting to a crime that I did not commit. Over and over again, I heard the exact same advice form hardened criminals that were familiar with the parole system.

When I finally met with the parole board, I was greeted with an all-too-familiar face at the video conference. Sitting there, right on the TV screen, was none other than the former chief of police, Joe Constance. The man who said I was going to break into houses and steal women's underwear. He was also the man who said that I needed to be locked up and put away even before I had a proper investigation or trial.

Lucky me. I looked around the room to see who else was there. I wouldn't have been surprised also to see the prosecutor who tried to give me 15 years in jail. It would just be my luck.

However, because of Joe's direct involvement with my incarceration, the parole hearing was adjourned for a later date.

It took months before another board was set up again to hear my parole. Luckily, the cards were not stacked against me this time, and I got a fresh new board. The hearing was going great. They saw my record in prison, saw that I had no previous arrests, and saw that I had taken all the classes I needed to. However, the moment came when they asked me the big question.

"Do you still say your innocent?"

All eyes were on me. It was as if time came to a standstill. Freedom seemed so close; I could feel it. All I had to was say that I was guilty, and I could walk out of this hell hole a free man.

"I did not commit the crime. I am innocent."

The words came out without hesitation. I would rather spend all my remaining days in jail than spend one day as a free man who admitted to a crime that I never committed.

The parole board members looked at each other and then finally look at me.

"We believe you," one of them said.

"Parole granted."

Tears ran down my face.

Someone actually believed me. Their belief in my innocence felt even better than the thought of leaving the prison system as a free man.

It was my Rocky moment.

I could hear the theme song to the movie playing in my ears as I walked down the corridor to the prison gates. My time in jail was done, but the memory and indignity of it will last forever.

Free at last. Free at last.

Thank God almighty. I'm free at last!

CHAPTER 6
SLAVE TO THE PAROLE SYSTEM

It was a good feeling to get back home and see my mother and kids once again. However, the justice system still had me on a tight leash. Though it had been 7 years since this nightmare began, I had another 14 whole years to go under the parole system. It's like the legal system was some sort of gang that did not want one of its members to leave. They still were watching over me, and I still had to play by their rules.

During my parole, there were some really demeaning rules like I could not be around kids, even my own, without another adult accompanying me. Imagine wanting to go with your teenage son to the movies or shopping and needing to ask your mom or a friend to come with you? It was a real pain, but that's what I had to do.

Some other stipulations that got under my skin were that I had to regularly attend counseling sessions, and that I was not allowed to leave the state without a special permit. It certainly beats being in prison but going and speaking to a counselor about sex crimes and sexual misconduct was just degrading. The whole process made me feel like a kid or worse yet, a slave to the system.

Here I am, a man without any previous legal offenses, being lectured to by some state appointed counselor on how not to be a pervert. It was humiliating to sit there week after week and discuss sex crimes that I never committed.

What really annoyed me was how the counselor always wanted me to admit to the crime that put me behind bars. I never understood why this woman was so insistent on me admitting guilt. It never made any sense. I did my time already.

These counseling sessions were like adding insult to injury, and I never really knew where she was going with her line of questioning until about 14 whole years into my parole. At that time, she sat me down and told me that in order to be successfully rehabilitated from my crime, I had to admit my guilt.

I thought this lady must be crazy or something. What was once a request by her now was an order.

As nice as I could, I told her that I will never admit to a crime that I did not commit.

That did not sit well with her. In fact, she said that if I did not admit guilt, she would throw me out of counseling.

Under the circumstances, that should have sounded good. However, she knew that if I were no longer attending sessions with her, it would be a parole violation, and I could go back to jail. She not only knew it, but she also threatened me with it.

I told her if that is what she had to do, then do it; but I would not admit to any crime that I did not commit.

I was prepared to get arrested, and that night I

listened to Dr. Martin Luther King, Jr's sermon, *But if Not*. In the sermon, he talked about following God's law instead of man's law. I knew that I had to be true to God and myself instead of to the legal system.

And to no surprise, the counselor did as she promised. The next day, I received a call from my parole officer at 7 in the morning, telling me to come to the office. I was then promptly arrested and charged with the violating conditions of my parole, citing failure to admit guilt during counseling.

After 3 and a half years in prison and 14 years of an event-free parole, here I was looking at the possibility of another 6-12 months in jail and 14 more years of parole. It's like the parole board was out to destroy me.

I really felt as if it were some form of slavery.

My friends at the time would plead with me to tell them what they wanted to hear, even I didn't commit any crime.

"Do what they tell you to do," they would say. "It doesn't matter."

Honestly, it did matter. I would rather spend every single day of my life locked up in chains behind bars than spend one day as a free man that admitted to a crime that I never committed. Though I wanted this entire legal nightmare to end, I could never look at myself in the mirror again or look at my kids the same way if I gave a false confession.

In fact, I spent every cent I owned in order to fight my parole charges. In the end, I had no money, no possessions, and since I ended up being evicted from my apartment, nowhere to live.

I didn't care. They could take everything I owned from me. However, they could not take my dignity.

After three 3 court hearings, the final judge ruled in my favor. During the hearing, he could not believe that I was essentially being tried for a crime which I already did time for. It was double jeopardy, and it was illegal under the law.

He said the charges had no merit and told me that I could finish my parole without having to admit to any crime.

Amen!

After 14 years of parole, 3 and a half years of prison, and 3 and a half years leading up to my first court case, it was a total of 21 years of my life lost. What the legal system did was wrong. No man should be subjected to such unjust treatment and harassment. This is America.

If ever there needed to be real prison reform, it was now. No man ever deserves the type of treatment I had to endure for this 21-year period. It was both unjust and unfair.

In addition to being disappointed with the entire legal system, I was disillusioned with the so-called black activists who promised to be there for the people. When I contacted Larry Hamm with The People's Organization for Progress, the man actually hung up the phone on me after I told him my predicament. He didn't give me the time of day. He promoted himself as an activist for the down-trodden and openly promoted prison reform.

Well, here I was, one ex-prisoner, and he wanted nothing to do with me. He didn't even have the courtesy to say no or that he couldn't help. I got no better treatment from Reverend Toby Sanders. The man of God flat out told me I was on my own because I spoke out previously about his political friends.

Shouldn't this preacher do what was ethically right and not worry what was politically expedient?

Hell no, I guess. His allegiance seemed to be to the law of man and not to that of God.

A guy never knows who his true friends are until he gets into trouble. Then, the truth comes out.

CHAPTER 7
BLACKBALLED

If I thought the legal system would be the only ones giving me problems after leaving jail, I was rudely surprised by the homecoming I received after moving back to Trenton. A leaper infected with Covid-19 would have been more welcomed in that city than I was.

It was as if I were the worst person that ever walked the planet. People would call me "Chester the Molester", rapist, and all sorts of names. Men and women would scream at me out the windows and yell the worst obscenities.

The honest truth was they were all ignorant. No one really knew the truth, and what made matters worse was the fact no one cared about the truth any way.

The word on the street was that I molested or raped a group of children and was some sort of deranged pervert. What was ironic was that I was never accused of these crimes. However, since the whispering that went on behind my back repeated the same false narrative, the people all ignorantly believed what they heard was true.

Glen Beck use to always say, "Don't believe me. Go look it up yourselves."

However, nobody looked anything up. Most people thought since they heard that I was some child rapist from their friends or other family members, it must be true. They were like a bunch of blind sheep being helplessly led around, not thinking or doing for themselves.

In the end, I felt sorrier for them than I did for myself.

At least I had a brain and could think. I had a least a chance of doing something better with my life or doing something important.

On many occasions, I would have bricks or bottles thrown at me. Even the local drug dealers ganged up on me one time and tried to beat me up. Here they are destroying the community and ruining kids' lives, and they had the audacity to try to run me out of town.

These guys were the biggest enemies of the entire city. If anyone needed to leave, they should be first in line.

In fact, one time, a gang member came up to me with a lead pipe and wanted to bash my head in. I was with my daughter. Just before he attacked me, my daughter began to cry, worried about the safety of her father.

The thug finally came to his senses and fled the scene. However, the trauma of the event still lingers with my daughter to this day.

Many people wondered why I stayed in Trenton.

It's not a bad question, but the honest answer was that Trenton was my home. My mother lived there, and more importantly the city still needed help. Plus, no one was going to ever make me leave this city unless I wanted to leave it.

Also, I wanted to prove something to them and to myself. I was not what the court said I was. I was not what the parole board said I was. And I certainly was not what the drug dealer, and his family said I was.

I still had a lot of good in me, and there was a lot of good that I needed to do.

However, this positive attitude only went so far when I was trying to find a job. Most places in town would see my name and not even consider hiring me. They feared what would happen to their business if people knew Daryl Brookes were working there.

Also, finding a good paying job was even more difficult because many businesses required background checks. I was turned down for all the city and state jobs I applied for as a result. Also, certain other big corporations rejected me after they saw I had a sexual assault charge on my record.

It's not like I wasn't qualified for these positions or even did poorly on the job interviews. In fact, most of these places loved me, and I would have been hired until they investigated my background.

It's like the shame of a crime that I never committed followed me around wherever I went.

Even when I got a job at certain places, I was fired once the owner knew my history. On more than one occasion, after a customer complained to the boss that I was working there, I was let go.

I remember one of the most degrading times when this occurred was while I was working behind the counter at Quiznos making sandwiches. I can recall as clear as day when one of my fellow black community activists came to the counter and pointed directly at me.

"I don't want this man making my food," she demanded, speaking to the owner.

Because she was a woman of stature in the community, I was fired on the spot and asked to leave immediately. It was one of the most humiliating events of my life. It was discrimination at its worst. At that moment, I truly felt the pain of all the black men and women in history who were discriminated against.

It was as if she were saying to me that I could not drink from thae water fountain or sit on the same seat on the bus where she drank or sat. I felt worthless and less than human at that moment and am sure that's exactly how the people discriminated in the past felt like.

It was difficult to maintain a stable job as a result. I was also left with working at places that did not conduct background checks or kept me out of the public eye. Therefore, I worked much of the time in the back of restaurants, making food where no one could see me. Luckily, I knew how to cook well, and no one ever complained of the food I made.

Working my ass off behind the stove at least paid the bills and put food on the table for me and my kids. It was not glamorous, but it was work. And I'd rather work than have my hand out asking the government for their help.

I wanted to go back to school and further my education at the time. However, with lower paying jobs, most of the time I had difficulty even trying to pay my former student loans as opposed to getting new ones. It would have been nice to get back to college at this stage of my life and move onto a different career path. But my time had not come yet.

Instead of paying for classes, I was able to attend free conferences, lectures, and seminars that the local colleges had to offer. Whether they were political in nature, about world affairs, or African American studies, they were all interesting, and I could not get enough of them. Luckily, Princeton University, Mercer County Community College, and Rider College all had these opportunities. Plus, I was able to use their libraries and read their books and magazines.

However, one by one, my past caught up to me at each of these alleged centers for higher education and understanding. At Mercer County Community College, a place where I was once highly respected, they rejected me. I not only was the VP of the student government, but I also was the president of the Black Student Union. They should have at least given me some consideration. Instead, they posted pictures of me at the security stations, and the local security staff were told to escort me off campus on sight.

I was so appalled by the treatment and lack of respect for one of their alumni that I went up to the Provost of the school, Monica Weaver, and asked what was going on. Ironically, this woman of higher education and stature gave the same ignorant response as the uneducated Trenton locals that I grew up with. She had the gall to tell me that I was a rapist and no longer a person that the college wishes to be associated with.

She never investigated the facts, researched the court cases, or knew anything about my incarceration. Despite my pleas of innocence, she wanted to hear no more of me or of my story.

At Rider College, the dean turned on me after an incident on campus. While discussing political and social issues with some of the students, one of their employees who worked as a cook there sold me out in the middle of a conversation that I was having with them.

This woman took it upon herself to say, "Do you know who this guy is? He is a child molester!"

Here I was, minding my own business, when a black woman who I did not know from Trenton came up to me and 3 college students and bad-mouthed me in front of them. I could not have been more embarrassed. I was completely caught off-guard and shocked. I was at a total loss for words. The students who I was speaking with at the time all looked at me with such disdain on their faces.

Who was she to get into my business and try to ruin my life? She was supposed to be my neighbor, my fellow black sister, fighting the system and watching out for her fellow man. However, she too turned on me.

That night I went home with such a deep depression and anger about the event. Though I was incensed about how the woman who came up to me, I was even more depressed at how the students looked at me.

My treatment at Princeton was no different. After spending some time on campus, one of the professors of African American Studies, Dr. Cornel West, called me into his office and told me that the African American Studies students did not want me coming to any of their programs any longer. Though he appreciated my activism, the students just didn't want me there.

It wasn't until one of my parole board meetings that the implications of that conversation surfaced. During the meeting, a note was handed to my parole officer by the head of Princeton University security. It was a persona non grata letter that was filed against me by the university. I was no longer welcomed on their campus ever again. The security guard told both me and my parole officer that if I stepped foot on Princeton again, I would be arrested.

I was so hurt that I literally broke down and cried.

"Why me, "I lamented. "I never did anything wrong on campus."

This time, it wasn't some random dean or provost that had a beef with me. Instead, it was my own people who rejected me. Ignorance had no educational or economic boundaries. What made matters worse was that this particular African American Studies program at Princeton was advocating for prison reform and prisoner's rights.

Here I was, someone who was in the prison system, did my time, and now was trying to better my life; and these Princeton students wanted nothing to do with me.

The stigmata and shame were not confined to the secular but spilled over into the so-called religious domain also. My own parish, Shiloh Baptist Church, proved just as unwelcoming. Comically, it reminded me of the movie *Forrest Gump*. Remember the scene when Forrest was on the bus and trying to get a seat? All the kids there would say the empty seat was taken, or the person sitting there would not allow him to sit next to them.

Well, the treatment I received was no different, and these folks were supposedly God-fearing people who were Christians. During church, no one wanted me to sit next to them and gave excuses why I should not sit in their pew. Some were polite while others simply told me that they did not want to be associated with me.

I was therefore left up in the balcony, sitting all by myself much of the time. Even the few people who came up there to worship did not want to sit next to me. Well, I came to church first and foremost to be with God, and I was not going to let them run me out of my own place of worship.

Even the Deacons could not convince me to leave, despite their request. Can you believe so-called men of God would ask someone to leave a place of worship because of a criminal record? Hell, the church was already full of criminals who already did jail time. Plus, known drug dealers attended services there on a regular basis. Worse yet, the most corrupt people who ever lived in the city, the mayor, congressmen, and council members, all attended Shiloh Baptist and were never asked to leave.

Like adding gasoline to the fire, the church's own secretary had placed a picture of me on her door for everyone to see who passed by her office. I'm not sure if she did it herself or if the reverend of Shiloh Baptist made her do it. However, all I knew was that my face was plastered in a news article for everybody who entered the church to see and read.

I was once an associate minister of the church under Reverend S. Howard Woodson before my incarceration. Now, wherever I went in the building, security would follow me around as if I were some sort of sexual predator.

What was even more ironic was that if asked, most of the people who attended services at the church thought that I was a child rapist. It seems you can preach away sin, but you can't preach away ignorance.

The thing that hurt me the most was how my oldest daughter was treated at school. It's one thing to call me names. However, it's a completely different story when those named are thrown at my own daughter. Nothing hurts a father more than when his child is hurting in any way. Worse yet, she was hurting not because of what she did, but it was because of what I supposedly did.

How sad was I when she would come home from school and say, "Daddy, the kids at school are making fun of me because of you again."

How upsetting for me was it to hear, "Daddy, why do all the kids call you such bad names?"

What do you say to your daughter? How do you respond to such a situation? Her pain ate me away on the inside for years.

Worse yet, I was not welcomed at school events. Plus, I feared that if I went, my daughter would get teased even more. I wanted to come to the school to talk to the principal about the problem. However, she once called me to say it would be better if I just stayed at home.

Watching her suffer made me suffer even more.

Kids were mean, and the parents were just as mean. You know the old saying, "The apple doesn't fall far from the tree." Well, no apples were rolling away from any trees here in Trenton. The teasing and mocking unbelievably lasted up to and even during her time in high school.

Luckily, she was the only one of my kids who received this treatment. And I thank God that she turned out to be a beautiful, successful, and well-adjusted young lady, despite what she went through earlier in life.

As a single man, finding a date also became a little challenging at times. For instance, once I found this really nice church-going young lady who I got along with well. We'd spend a lot of our free time together and really enjoyed being with each other. Plus, she found me funny, and no matter how bad the joke I told, she would always laugh.

Everything was going well until she brought me home to have dinner with her parents. As soon as I walked through the door, it was as if I had 2 heads or something. I guess my girlfriend never told them who I was. However, when they saw me, they obviously knew my history. Her parents stared me down the whole night and gave me the coldest of shoulders.

The dinner went so bad that I can remember having better times at a funeral than I did spending time with her parents.

In the end, they forbid her from seeing me again, and the friendship ended. She later died of heart failure. Damn!

It's times like this when the world seems to close in on you. Though I do not suffer from depression, there were certain days or times of the day when I felt as if it were trying to set in.

However, I quickly got out of these states of funk by listening to old sermons by Dr. Martin Luther King, Jr. The words he spoke were just as powerful as they were back then as they are to me now.

Truth forever on the scaffold. Wrong forever on the throne. Yet that scaffold sways the future, and behind the dim unknown standeth God within the shadow, keeping watch above His own.

No oppressor ever transforms and shows empathy toward his target. The victim has to draw a line himself and firmly let the oppressor know that any disrespectful behavior won't be tolerated.

Words like these would quickly bring me out of my self-induced sadness and back to reality. I knew God still had good for me to do in this world. I knew that I had much more to offer, and I was not going to let the people around me, no matter what they say, rule my life.

Fate can be a mysterious thing. You never know when or where it will strike. However, when it calls, you must be willing and ready to react.

Just such a moment occurred when I was walking home one afternoon. In the distance, I saw what looked like a homeless man collapse on the ground. Other people in the street just looked at him and did nothing. However, this gentleman obviously seemed to be in distress. His face was blue, and he did not appear to be breathing.

The man was dying right in front of our eyes, but no one around him was doing anything. They just stared at the man.

That's just not right.

I instantly dropped to my hands and knees and started CPR while I asked this random man to call 911. Luckily, the ambulance arrived within 15 minutes, and the man was whisked away to St. Francis Medical Center.

I felt bad for the gentleman and assumed that he

probably had no friends or family. The thought of him dying in the hospital alone, without at least one person around him who cared, just seemed sad. I therefore went straight to the hospital and waited outside his room, expecting the worst.

While there, I learned that the man was not homeless, but had a family and a nice place to live. His name was Joseph McNamara, and he was a state union representative. I got to meet his family after they arrived at the hospital. It was heartwarming how these people treated me. This suburban, Irish family made me feel as if I were one of the family, and they welcomed me as if I were their long-lost son.

The gentleman finally awoke, but because of his extensive heart damage, he passed away a few weeks later. The real blessing to the story was that the CPR I gave to him allowed the man to live love enough so that his family could say their goodbyes.

A "I love you" made his passing that much easier on his family. And as a result, they were forever grateful for the selfless act of mercy I performed that day on the streets of Trenton.

To this day, I still keep in touch with them. In fact, I feel as if the man's wife became like a second mother to me and her 2 sons were like my newfound brothers. Below is a picture of me with the family:

Plus, Mrs. McNamera was there for me later when the parole board was trying to send me back to prison. I'd like to share the note she wrote to them on my behalf:

Daryl M. Brooks and Stephen Martino

Trenton NJ, 08625   November 9, 2016

Re: Darryl Brooks

To Whom It May Concern:

My first contact with Darryl Brooks was the evening of June 16th, 2016 at St. Francis Medical Center, Trenton. He had intervened in my husband, Joseph's, life that morning. Approximately 9:30 AM, my husband was walking from one business meeting to another near the Capital building, when he collapsed on the street. Per witnesses, a crowd surrounded him, one woman said he was turning blue, a man asked if anyone knew CPR, Darryl stepped forward. He knelt on the sidewalk giving Joseph CPR until the EMT's and police arrived. He did get a slight pulse, the EMT's used a defibulator to keep his heart going. Joseph was taken by ambulance to St Francis. Darryl followed him to the ER, per one of the nurses. He told her, he didn't want Joseph to be alone. He stayed for hours. I finally arrived near 2PM, the nurse told me that Darryl had saved my husband's life by preforming CPR. She called him a "good Samaritan" and that his name was Darryl Brooks.

Joseph was moved from the ER to cardiac intensive care, while in his room that evening, a young man stood in the doorway, appearing quite sad. As I walked toward him, he told me his name. I was overwhelmed with joy, jumped up and hugged him, telling him I loved him for saving my husband's life. During the week Joseph was in this hospital, Darryl came to visit daily, he was very concerned. He and my sons exchanged contact information, Darryl would send a text each morning to get an update. Due to Darryl stepping forward on the 16th, we did have one day when my husband was lucid enough to know us, we are grateful for that.

On June 24th, Joseph was airlifted to Lourdes Medical Center, Camden. While here, we heard from Darryl daily, expressing his concern for Joseph and us. He felt a loss when we told him on July 1st that Joseph was removed from life support.

Darryl did something very special for our family, giving us the ability to have a few more days with Joseph. We have continued our contact with Darryl, he has visited our home, he is a wonderful, compassionate man. I'm proud to consider him a friend and wish him all my best. We can never express how thankful we are for his being that "good Samaritan."

Sincerely,
Ellen M McNamara

RECEIVED
NOV 1 4 2016
SPECIAL HEARING UNIT
OFFICE OF THE PUBLIC DEFENDER

70

CHAPTER 8
BORN ACTIVITST

Did you ever feel as if you had a calling in life? For some people maybe it is to play sports; for others it's to go into a certain profession. Well, for me, I always knew God put me on this planet to be an activist and fight for the people who couldn't fight for themselves and speak for the people who couldn't speak for themselves.

Even when I went to college, I was really interested in how the world worked, the different people who lived in it, and how to make the planet a better place. It's not like some pie in the sky dream I had as a kid. This belief that I would become an activist and make a real change in the world has been with me since day 1.

As I said previously, I advocated as a child to keep the local library open and always spoke up about social injustices in my town. I never held back. Being popular was not my motivation. However, doing what was right always was.

When I talk about activism, I'm speaking of the old-school, Dr. Martin Luthor King, Jr. type of activism.

Passive protests, marches, and dissemination of information to the public were my ways of making a change. I wanted to make where I lived a better place and not destroy it like I see these "so-called" activists of today doing to their cities. Hell, how can you make your home and the people's lives in it a better place if you are burning down the whole damn town?

Plus, the passive Dr. Martin Luthor King, Jr. type of protests brought positive news to the situation. It was an effective way to make a point and a peaceful method to achieve your goals.

One of the first protests I ran was when I was the Black Student Union president at Mercer County Community College. In Trenton, there was this Hispanic-operated store that would run the little black kids out of it or treat them very poorly. What was ironic was that the store was in the middle of a predominantly black neighborhood, and their customers were predominantly black.

It didn't make sense. So, I sent in a few kids with some money to see what happened. Instead of buying something, these kids were rudely asked to leave. That didn't sit well with me.

As a result, I organized a protest with some of the local kids and their mothers. That day, we lined the street where the business was located and shut it down for about 4 hours. My goal was not to hurt anyone who lived there or prevent anyone from walking or shopping on the road. I just wanted people to become aware of the situation.

The protest worked and no one ever had a problem with the store again.

With this 1990 protest, I gained considerable notoriety as a community organizer and as someone who could actually make a difference in the city. The following year, the black student union from Rider College called me up and asked for me to stage a protest on their campus. Because some of the Rider students were from Trenton, they thought of me when looking for a person to head up this event.

The union wanted to protest one of the fraternities who had held an event called "N—Night". During this event, all the college kids got dressed up as if they were from the hood and painted their faces black. It was highly offensive to all the black students on campus. However, the fraternity decided to have the event despite polite requests not to.

I was honored to lead the charge. On the day of the protest, I walked hand and hand with the president of the college, along with 300 other protesters, up to the fraternity. The entire campus was shut down for the event, and it made the headlines of all the local papers.

When I reached the fraternity, I went inside and spoke with the president of the organization. He was a nice kid and apologized. However, because of the racial damage caused by his party, the president kicked the fraternity off campus. Also, because of our protest, there have been no further racist-type of events ever held at the college again.

It was ironic that the same college that I had helped fight racial justice turned its back on me 25 years later. It's amazing how quickly people forget.

I also spent much of my time organizing events such as "Stop the Violence", "Stop Police Brutality", and "Stop the Guns" while I was living in Trenton. I regularly held well-attended marches, gave lectures, and generated public awareness on the situations that affected our local city. People loved them, and the politicians all wanted to show their faces at them. I was also honored to work with Kathy McBride during these events. She was, at that time, the head of Mothers Against Violence.

I was tired of the poverty, guns, and street violence. I was tired of police brutality. I'm not saying that all cops awere bad, but the few bad apples in the bunch stuck out like a sore thumb. More importantly, I was tired of the poor education system the city offered to the young people.

I took my message to the air with a radio show called *Live with Daryl Brooks* four nights a week on WTTM AMM. It became so popular that Comcast gave me my own public access show and named it with the same title.

My message was going out to the people, and more importantly, they were listening. On my shows, I'd host special guests and have people call in. I spoke up against the crooked political system in Trenton and let the people know what was really happening in our city. For some, it was the first time they actually heard real news and not what was manufactured or spoon-fed to them by the politicians or traditional media outlets.

The first step to make change is to educate the people about the problem and provide solutions to make them better. My message took off, and people, for once, became aware of what was going on in their neighborhoods.

The politicians also became aware of what I was saying, especially when I mentioned them by name and called them out for their incompetence and corruption. First of all, most of the guys who were in office weren't there because they were qualified but got there because of local popularity or as a favor. Just because a person is popular, doesn't mean they know how to run a city.
I'm not saying all of the politicians were corrupt, but a bunch of them became that way when they got into government. It's like the power and prestige of the office corrupted them.

As a result, I became unpopular with the politicians who ran city, especially when I was asking the tough questions. They never liked it when I asked them where all the money that was earmarked by the local and state government for our city was going. I knew it wasn't going to promote jobs, education, or any building projects.

On many of my shows, I explained to my audience where the money was going. Just like Glenn Beck's television program, I exposed the crony capitalism that ran our city. Instead of the funds heading to where they belonged, some of the money went to creating 6-figure government jobs as a payoff or as a political favor. As the money came into the city, much of it would be distributed among the politicians themselves instead of to the people.

I was making enemies quickly as a result. It reminded me of Dr. Martin Luthor King, Jr. when he started to lose his popularity. It was all fine and dandy when he was doing his marches and sit-ins. However, when he talked politically and spoke out against the Vietnam War, that's when the politicians took it personally. Unlike getting thrown in jail for speaking out against the system, he ended up 6 feet underground.

I never said being an activist was a glorious job. However, someone needs to do it. And if God put me on this planet to be an activist and make a change, then he will give me the strength and determination to overcome all that the opposition has to throw at me.

As I said before, I wanted to follow in Dr. Martin Luthor King, Jr.'s footsteps. As a result, I joined the Southern Christian Leadership Conference (SCLC). King was both a member and its first president. I went to their conferences and even had a chance to march with them for their 40th anniversary walk in honor of the march from Selma to Montgomery, Alabama. There, I had an opportunity to become friends with great civil rights leaders like Harry Belafonte, Reverend Al Sampson, James Orange, and James Bevel along with Dr. Bernard Lafayette.

From them, I received motivation and learned what it takes to become a true activist. These men took what they were believing in to a whole level and put most other activists, such as the ones in Trenton, to shame. These men peacefully did what they needed to do in order to create meaningful change. They disregarded politics and even themselves for the good of a greater cause.

They taught me that the pendulum swings in all things in life. For example, who would have thought that after Dr. King was shot, he would be honored the way he is today? People forget how unpopular he was after he died, especially after coming out against the Vietnam War. Now, there is a holiday named after him, roads dedicated to him, and schools around the country teach about him as part of their regular curriculum.

These preachers would quote the late reverend by recalling his words.

God is on the side of truth and justice. Good Friday may occupy the throne for a day, but ultimately it must give way to the triumph of Easter. Evil may so shape events that Caesar will occupy a palace and Christ a cross, but that same Christ arose and split history into B.C. and A.D., so that even the life of Caesar must be dated by his name. Yes, "the arc of the moral universe is long, but it bends toward justice." There is something in the universe which justifies William Cullen Bryant in saying, "Truth crushed to earth will rise again."

Just look at how the pendulum has swung. Back in the 1960's, J. Edgar Hoover was on the throne. He was the man in charge while Dr. King was considered the outsider and by some, a nobody. But look at how the tables have turned. Many kids have never heard of the name Hoover, and if they did, it probably wasn't positive. However, Dr. King is a man known and beloved throughout the country and the world.

The people from the SCLC told me than when God is on your side, things will eventually go your way.

Inspired by the time I spent with my brothers from the Southern Christian Leadership Conference, I brought my message back to the streets. Something needed to be done about the gang violence, the killings, and the endless shootings that plagued the entire city of Trenton. It's not that the police weren't going after the criminals, but the real issue was stopping the crimes before they were even committed.

One of the main issues I tackled in 2006 was the easy access to ammo. Virtually anyone could get their hands on it, and at Dick's Sporting Goods, all you needed was a valid license to purchase some. You didn't even have to have a gun license to purchase ammo at Dick's. A regular driver's license or other valid form of ID was all that was needed. It meant any dude off the street could basically walk in and buy a case of ammo. No questions asked.

When cops went to arrest the murderers and raid gang houses, boxes upon boxes of Dick's ammo were routinely found throughout their places. It was no secret where the ammo was coming from. However, despite this problem staring the cops and the politicians directly in their faces, no one did a single thing about it.

That's not right.

People were always complaining of gun control. However, if you don't have any bullets, the gun becomes useless.

I therefore organized a peaceful sit-in protest at one of the local Dick's Sporting Goods Stores to demonstrate against their easy-to-purchase ammo policy. Hundreds came out to support the cause and surrounded the store for hours in protest. All business there came to a standstill.

That day could not have been any colder. We all felt as if we were going to freeze to death. I thought people were going to give up the instant the cold wind and frigid weather hit their faces. However, we all stood tall and held our ground, praying frostbite wouldn't set in.

Dick's agreed to our demands and changed their policy. Instead of just needing any old license, a person buying ammo now needed to provide a valid handgun license. This was a huge step in the right direction. In order to get a handgun license, there was a background check and validation protocol completed by trained professionals at the police department.

This policy was taken statewide and proved to be a huge success.

Along with local politics, I tried to bring my activism to a state level. How else better to do this than to run for office. I know it sounds odd to be on parole and run for office, but that's what I did.

Running for NJ State Congress twice, once as a Green Party member and the other as an Independent, and State Senate once, I brought my message to a much higher level. It was not about winning at that time. I knew that I didn't have the funds or the political backing. It was all about the messaging and disseminating my thoughts and ideas to the people and to the other candidates. Below is a picture of me taking my message to the streets:

After living in Trenton for most of my life, I had given up on the Democratic Party. Well, let me rephrase that. It's not like I gave up on them. They became too corrupt and gave up on me and the people that they were elected to serve.

At first, I went from the Green Party to the Independent Party. However, I really found my first political home with the Libertarians. Unlike the Democrats, they were not corrupted. They were the real peoples' party who represented the common man and woman of America. Plus, their political platform sat well with me.

The idea of less government seemed like a godsend, especially after coming from Trenton. Plus, they spoke of the power of the individual and of personal freedom. The thought that people made the country great, not the government, was certainly a welcome message. These were real people who cared more about the American citizen than they did about the power.

Though I made a lot of friends within the

organization and went to many of their events, I was eventually drawn to the Tea Party movement. I'm not saying that I completely left the Libertarians. However, this new movement was full of Libertarians along with Republicans and even Democrats. I was so fascinated with the group that I went to their 2009 9/12 rally that was held in Washington, DC.

Both my mother and friends warned me not to go. They said they would lynch me and that the group was nothing but racists.

From the moment I met them, I never saw one ounce of racism. And the mere thought of them lynching anyone was completely absurd.

From day one, the press gave the Tea Party a bad reputation, and the people of Trenton and many throughout the country believed it. The mainstream media had it out for the group and singlehandedly wanted to destroy the movement before it even took root. Because they didn't believe in what the Tea Party was preaching, they villainized them and anyone who joined them. Black or white, they put you in their crosshairs.

Just belonging to the Tea Party, I was called a racist, an "Uncle Tom", and a sellout.

That's what the media does when they disagree with you or your organization. Instead of reporting the facts or investigating the truth, they call you names and demonize you if they disagree with your political point of view. It's a shame what has happened to America's mainstream media. Unfortunately, many people bought the media's storyline as if it were gospel. To them, the Tea Party movement was nothing more than a bunch of redneck racists who wanted to go back to the Jim Crow days.

If the group were so racist, how did I become one of the leaders of the organization? I guess they didn't hate black people that much if they let me run the show. Below is me proudly speaking out at a rally:

When I was a member of the Tea Party, it was the first time I saw white people go after other white people. While growing up, I was made to believe that white people only went after black people. That was not the case at all. The Tea Party challenged anyone who was not abiding by the Constitution of the United States. That was the rule of the land, and many politicians forgot about this original mandate which created our great nation.

Their challenge was not confined to the Democrats, they went after Republicans also, especially the ones referred to as Rino's (Republican in name only). The Tea Party really cared about the United States and the people who lived in it. They did not want to see the power-hungry politicians in charge destroy our country in the name of progress while financially becoming wealthy in the process.

Just look at Nancy Pelosi. She's worth over 200 million dollars. How can you make that kind of money on less than $200,000 dollars a year? Well, you don't have to think hard to figure it out. These national politicians were just as corrupt as the local ones, and the Tea Party knew it.

I always called politicians like Pelosi "Good Time Charlies". Sure, they will promise you all sorts of things, and tell you what you want to hear. Hell, they'd say anything and promise anything to get into office. They'd get up on a platform and act like if you voted for them, everything would be perfect. It would be a good time for everyone, and we'd all be living in a utopia.

They didn't care about the people. They were just using them to get into power and promote their own interests.

Again, look at Nancy Pelosi. If she were such a great politician, San Francisco would be the greatest place to live in the world.

Just look at the city. It's a dump. Hell, the fraternity filled with dried beer and piss that I got kicked off Rider College smelled better than the district she's supposed to represent.

We have all this great technology and scientific knowledge here in America. We can put a man on the moon, treat all sorts of cancer, and have computers now that are smarter than anyone who has ever lived. Yet, we cannot not fix the simple problems which plague our cities. How can that be possible?

I can tell you. The problem comes from the top. If these politicians wanted to make a change or turn their cities, such as San Francisco, into the best place to live on the planet, they have every means in the world to do so. However, they don't.

And that was why the people in power feared the

Tea Party. They were the ones calling them out for their hypocrisy, and they were the ones getting to the root of the problem. That's why the politicians sicked the media on them. They posed a real threat, and that threat was growing and appealing to more people.

As a leader of the Tea Party, I met other leaders throughout the state and country. I also attended meetings, held events, and was a frequent speaker for the group. At these events, I talked politics on a national and global level. It was so refreshing to get out of that tiny Trenton bubble where people only cared about what was happening in their city and to discuss much broader topics such as foreign affairs and issues that affected the entire country. It broadened my horizons, and I met lifelong friends as a result.

Also, my Tea Party friends were the one's there for me when I lost my mother to cancer. As an only child, the responsibility of taking care of her when she was sick was my sole responsibility. There was no one else, and my mother needed help. Because of the radiation and chemotherapy, the treatments weakened her. Plus, the cancer itself made it difficult for her to care for her daily needs.

As a result, I moved in with her and stayed by her side, both day and night, except the little time when I went to work. I could not let my mother die alone.

After she passed, I was financially broke. Plus, the Trenton Housing Authority evicted me from her apartment 3 days after her death. I found out this "good news" by going to the apartment door and noting that my key would not work. With nowhere to go, I moved into a hotel.

Kamau Kujichagulia and my other close friends helped me initially pay for the room. However, after running out of money for rent, my girlfriend told me to turn to God for help. Getting down on my knees, I prayed for help.

God is great and he answered my prayers in the name of the Tea Party.

I reached out to Barbara Gonzalez from their Bayshore chapter. She put out my cause on her Facebook group. One of the members of the group called me up and said, "I know your struggle. I know what you've been through."

She then gave me $1,100 dollars.

In total, the Facebook message ended up collecting $1,700 dollars for me.

Thank you, Jesus.

Using these funds, I got my own apartment and was soon able to obtain a good paying, fulltime job.

The people who were calling the Tea Party racists obviously never knew the same people I did. In fact, I doubt they ever wanted to meet any of them. It was all too easy to label the group with derogatory names instead of learning who they were and what they believed in.

I also thank God for my long-time girlfriend, Jaunlette, who has forever changed my life. She was the person who took me to see my mother in the hospital the day she died. She was there for me when I had to make the difficult decision to take her off of life support. She was the woman standing by my side in the room as my mother passed away.

I think it was a matter of fate that we met in the first place. Maybe it was God or maybe it was luck, but I feel as if we were destined to be together forever. I can remember the first time we met. I was working in a bookstore in Philadelphia.

Just as I finished my shift, I saw this young lady in the distance and wanted to give her my phone number.

Hastily, I wrote down the number and ran after her. However, she had vanished as if she were some sort of a spirit. No matter where I looked, I could not find her. What was odd was the fact that one minute she was right in front of me and the next, she was gone.

While looking for her, I caught the riverline train. As I entered one of the cars, I looked up and saw the most beautiful smile that I had ever seen in my life. It was the not the smile from the woman I was looking for, but it was the smile I had been waiting for all my life. In that instant, I felt an instant attraction. It was like nothing I had ever felt in my life nor was it like anything I have ever felt since that time. I knew my life was changed forever.

Maybe that woman I saw in the distance was an angel, leading me towards my destiny. I will never know; but what I do know is that was when I first met Jaunlette. Below is a picture of her and I:

After introducing myself, I handed her the phone number that I had written. We started dating soon after, but within 5 months, the relationship ended. Despite the breakup, I could not stop thinking about her. For some reason, I knew we were meant to be together. During this time, I did date other women and ended many relationships without thinking twice about it.

My mind, however, always went back to Jaunlette. After years of being separated, I attempted to rekindle the relationship by sending her a few emails. After no response, I initially ended my pursuit, assuming that she just moved on with her life.

However, one night I was awoken by this urge to check my email. I never get up and check my email. In fact, when I go to bed, I stay there until I get up in the morning. This night I ran over to my computer and checked my messages. As if by fate, Jaunlette had returned one of the emails that I had sent her long ago.

Though it was almost 10 years since we had separated in 2003, it was as if no time at all had passed. Since that day, we have been almost inseparable. We camp, go on trips, laugh, and spend much of our free time together. I've never met any woman in my life like her before. She is the only other woman ever, other than my mother, that I would trust with my kids, my finances, and my life. When I think of her, these lyrics by Marvin Gay come to my mind:

> *Ooh, oh, how many eyes*
> *Have seen their dream*
> *Oh, how many arms*
> *Have felt their dream*
> *How many hearts, baby*
> *Have felt their world stand still?*

If I had 20 dollars to my name, I would spend it all

on flowers just for her. That's the kind of woman she is. I love to cook for her, be there for her during her times of need, and to tell her everything on my mind.

Though we have not tied the knot as of yet, she is the only woman in my life that I ever wanted to marry. It will happen. All in God's timing.

CHAPTER 9
GOING MAGA

When the 2016 presidential election came around, I was pulling day one for my boy Ted Cruz. He was the Tea Party's favorite. Plus, as a libertarian at heart, I loved his firm belief in the Constitution. He was our "golden child", and I thought he was going to be a sure win for the Republican nomination.

Plus, he was one of the nicest and most courteous politicians I had ever met. The first time I saw him face to face was during a protest in Washington, DC. All the candidates vying for the Republican nomination at that time were there to voice their disapproval over the Iran nuclear deal. It was a sour deal, and we all knew it.

During this event, I also met candidate Donald Trump. The man came down there not only looking like he had won the Republican nomination, but that he had also been elected president. He had a huge entourage with him at the time. I originally thought to myself, "What a cocky dude."

In fact, when Ted Cruz lost the nomination, my

enthusiasm for the entire election dwindled. Though I distrusted Hillary Clinton, Trump never really did it for me at first. I watched that "Trump train" go by and never boarded it. I said to myself, "I'll take the next one."

In fact, for that election, I found myself stumping for local politicians and never hit the streets for Trump. My friend, Lou Jasikoff, in Scranton, Pennsylvania needed help with his campaign. He was running for state representative and had asked me to help pull things together for him during the final few days before voting began.

On the night of the election, I found myself out in Scranton in a restaurant, watching the results come in. As one by one the states fell in Trump's favor, I said to myself, "That guy is actually going to do it."

I wasn't surprised, though, by the turn of events. While in Scranton, I personally witnessed long lines of people coming out to vote for him. It reminded me of the 2008 election when people stood for hours just to cast their ballot for Obama. There was no difference. The people all loved Trump and stood outside in the cold all day just to vote for him.

Plus, these were mostly Democrats. Scranton is a blue-collar, working-class town. It should have been a sure win for Hillary, but they weren't there for her. The Democrats had let the working folk down. The factories had left there just as they did in Trenton. The people were looking for a change.

While in Scranton, I got to meet and talk to a whole bunch of people. They were great. They opened up to me, and we talked about politics, the elections, and why they were voting for Trump. These were real people who had real concerns. Plus, they all couldn't have been friendlier.

I remember eating wings in the restaurant when the election was called by the media for Trump. The place went crazy. CNN was on at the time, and I can remember to this day watching Van Jones lambast the people of Scranton and other working-class areas of Pennsylvania. He called them racists and reprimanded them on the air.

Did he ever even meet someone from Scranton? Did he ever want to meet anyone from the working areas of Pennsylvania? I don't think so. If he did, he would have been singing a different tune.

I was in the town for days and never saw a shred of racism. While sitting in the restaurant on election night, I saw kids dressed in their LeBron James' jerseys, and the locals had no trouble talking to a 6-foot five black man from the hood as if I were one of them.

They got a raw deal that night.

It wasn't only CNN. All the other mainstream media outlets were in outrage. Instead of reporting the facts, they were name calling and blaming. You could tell they were angry. And what was worse, they were taking it out on both Trump and all the people who voted for him. They were labeling people who voted for Trump xenophobes, womanizers, racists, Nazis, and traitors. Trump had not even set foot into office, and the media meltdown had already begun. They never gave him a chance. Their hatred for the man started that night and never left for even a single day while he was in office.

If he'd say up, they would say down. If he made a peace accord with Israel, they would call him an anti-Semite. If he decreased black unemployment, they labeled him a racist. No matter what he said or did, it was wrong.

When I got back to Trenton, I remember sitting next to a woman on the riverline train. She was just coming back from the state house after protesting Trump. The man wasn't even in office and the protests had begun. I was really intrigued and asked her why she hated Trump so much. I was wondering what he could have done wrong when he wasn't even in office yet.

She had no answer for me. There was no particular policy she was against. In fact, she told me that she hoped that that he gets assassinated. I asked her if she would feel bad for his wife, children, or family if he died. I mean, I lost my mother and know how bad it feels if you lose a loved one. It's not fun.

What surprised me was that she had the audacity to say that she didn't even care about any of them.

"What type of movement was this?" I asked myself.

It's one thing to hate Trump, but now these people also hated his entire family. Plus, he hadn't even done anything as of yet. Just like the media, they never gave him a chance.

The people of Trenton were no different. The word on the street was that Trump was going to send them all back to Africa. Plus, they feared the Jim Crow laws may come back with him in office.

Now, where in hell did they get those ideas?

The whole thing was just insane. The media was going crazy and working all the people up into a crazed frenzy. They were the ones fueling the fire and putting nonsense into their minds.

I felt bad for the guy. In fact, Trump and I had a lot in common, and I felt his pain. The media attacked me the same way they did him. I remember the media coming down hard on me after my arrest and them just treating me like dirt when I was running for office. It was like they didn't like to see a black man with his own ideas who didn't conform to what they thought a man of color should believe in.

It wasn't fair what they did to me, and it wasn't fair what they were doing to Trump.

And it was nonstop. From the beginning, they reported on one made up problem after another. The presidency started with a bang after the Russia collusion hoax and the subsequent investigation. Then, there were other issues they fabricated such as the incident with Ukraine, the cages on the border, and Stormy Daniels, to name a few.

Hell. The media never got the story right, and it was one lie after another. The Russia collusion proved untrue after spending millions of US tax dollars. Obama made, built, and used the cages. In fact, the picture used by the news, showing the cages, were taken when Obama was still the president. Obama was the one who deported 4 million illegals. The Ukraine story also proved completely fake. In fact, the only thing it proved was that Biden and his crooked, crack-smoking son were crooks.

Trump had done nothing wrong, and the media painted him out to be the next boogieman. I guess they needed someone to hate. Guys like Osama Bin Laden and Muammar Gaddafi were already dead. Plus, Hitler was long gone, but they never failed to make the comparison. Trump was now public enemy number one, the new boogie man.

The longer he was in office, the more I enjoyed his presidency. Plus, whenever I had a chance, I would go out and speak on his behalf at different rallies and events. I went from not caring about him to being one of his biggest fans. The man was doing America good. Jobs were at an all-time high. No new wars were being started around the world. The economy was going great. Black unemployment was down.

What was there not to like? He said that he was going to make America great, and dammit, he was doing it.

I know people didn't like him as a person. However, we don't elect a president to be our moral leader. It's not like he's supposed to go to Rome and be the next Pope. If I wanted to elect a moral leader, I would vote for one of my pastors.

No. What you want is a businessman in office. Our country needs someone who knows how to run a company, not spiritually lead the nation. That's not his job.

That's why I can't believe when people say to me that Trump was the worst president ever. You telling me that he was worse than Carter or Bush junior? What did he do wrong in office? He loves this country and did everything he could do to make it a better place, more so than any other president in my lifetime. Plus, he kept his campaign promises.

People called him a liar.

That's simply not true. He said what he was going to do and did it.

Amen and God bless him and America for it!

CHAPTER 10
POLL WATCHING

During Trump's presidency, I moved to Philadelphia, Pennsylvania and became an active member of the Republican party there. After living in Trenton just about all of my life, I was now a Pennsylvania registered voter for the first time.

Just like Trenton, Philadelphia was another badly run city, filled with its own corruption and forgotten poor. My message of education reform, getting drugs off the streets, and reducing violence was just as needed there as it was for my own hometown.

Because of my previous experience with the polls during elections, the Republican party that I had been working with in the city called me up and asked me to be a poll watcher for the 2020 election.

I thought it would be a great idea. Because Trump was already warning the American people about a potential "cheat-by-mail" scheme that he suspected the Democrats would try to pull, I felt as if it were my moral obligation to go to the polls in order to ensure the integrity of the election. Without a fair and legal election, our democracy would be dead. Plus, I had been a poll watcher for other elections, including presidential ones. I knew the ropes and understood the entire process.

November 3, 2020 was a hugely anticipated day. All eyes across the world were now on the United States. Not only were they watching who would be the leader of the free world, but they were also interested to see if we could pull off a fair election. As we were the nation that touted democracy and that every person had their say in the government through a fair voting process, the world was ready to see if we practiced what we preached.

Plus, our whole country was in a frenzy about this election. The media had hyped it even before President Trump was first sworn into office. People were on the verge of riots and tension among Americans was at an all-time high. I felt like our entire country was a proverbial dam, just ready to burst.

I had high hopes about this election when I went down to the Philadelphia Convention Center that November day. Though I was rooting for Trump, I was rooting harder for the election process to be a fair one.
However, as soon as the counting began, there was a problem. Right off the bat, they kept me and the other poll watchers at a 20-foot distance. There was this designated line that we could not cross.

I've been doing elections for years and had never seen any line previously. Who had made this line, and why was it there? I asked many of the officials running the election why we were being kept from doing our job. However, there was no answers or explanations.

"That's the rules," and "That's how it is," was their only responses.

It didn't make any sense. I remembered being at

these events before, standing right next to the ballot counters. Plus, I was allowed to talk to them while they were counting and ask them questions. That was my job, and now I couldn't do it.

Hell, I couldn't do or see anything from 20 feet away. Having poll watchers there that could not do their jobs was a waste. Our presence at the convention center seemed like a mere formality so the Democrats could say with a big grin on their faces, "Yes, we allowed poll watchers during the counting, just as the law states."

Remember the 2000 election when they were recounting the votes? People were side by side inspecting the ballots. While one counted, others closely watched. That's the way it should be. That's the way it always was.

Plus, don't give me any of this COVID-19 BS. We weren't kept that far from them because of some virus. We were kept at a distance because they were hiding something. Plus, the people counting the votes and the officials never complied to any six-foot rule. They were all next to each other, doing their "jobs".

I tried to do my job the best that I could at that distance. I leaned over the lines to get a better look, and I even found some binoculars so I could get a see what was going on.

That Democrats did not take too kindly to my persistence. In fact, they called security on me 3 times, and I was forced to put away my binoculars. The officials there even came up to me in a rush and asked if I saw anything through them.

Now wasn't that ironic? These officials that were there to ensure the integrity of the election were suddenly worried that I saw something. What they were more concerned about was if the binoculars I was using had some sort of recording device in them.

After security and the officials inspected them, that was the end of my binoculars.

The other Democratic poll workers there were just as rude. They harassed me all day, trying to egg me on by saying, "As a black man, how could you work for Trump?"

They called me racist along with our president. Here, these white folks were calling the only black man there a racist. Weren't they supposed to be the party of understanding and racial equality? Well, there was none of that this day. No Republican poll watchers were harassing them, but they went out of their way to try to make my time there as miserable as it could be.

Another thing that I found fishy about this entire counting process were the bags of ballots coming through the doors. During previous election, just about all of the mail-in ballots were there already there. It was unusual to see anyone bringing in any more bags of ballots, and if they did, we were informed of exactly where they came from.

This time, in 2020, no one told us where any of these ballots were coming from. It was like they were falling from the sky and being collected to get counted. It's not like I didn't ask where they were coming from. In fact, I went up to all the officials I could find and demanded answers.

"Get behind the line," and "It's none of your business," were the only responses I got.

I told them that it is my business and the business of the entire United States of America to know where these bags were coming from. Instead of getting answers, they tried to shut me up. In the end, the guys running this whole charade would say, "It's official."

What's that supposed to mean?

Another thing I never got any answers about was why these election officials shut down the counting of the ballots in the middle of the night on the first day. This was not my first rodeo. No one ever shuts down the counting. And why did they shut it down just as President Trump took a convincing lead over Joe Biden?

There were other lawyers there asking the same question. They got the same response as they gave me.

None.

My mother didn't raise any fool. The Democrats were up to something, and that something came when the endless bags of mail-in votes began flooding through the doors.

It was like I was watching a horror movie, but instead of sitting there in my seat with some popcorn, I was living it. The entire country was living it. The fix was in, and I could do nothing about it. No one there could do a damn thing about it.

What was also not right about the entire process were the ballot counters themselves. Usually, the ones who count the ballots were well-trained city or state officials that have been through the whole process before. Unlike these usual ballot counters, the ones Philadelphia used came from a run-of-the-mill temp agency.

I personally spoke to the ballot counters during their breaks. None of them had ever done this job before, and the agency that sent them did not require any special background checks or training. They were all novices. The only thing that they were told to do was put the ballots that were opened into a machine to be counted.

They didn't care. They were getting paid, and if the officials told them to put the ballots in the machine, that's all they did. No more. No less.

The usual process was that when the ballot worker got a ballot in front of them, they would inspect its authenticity. They would then check the signature on it and check the person's name off a long list after the vote was counted. That was the protocol for every election that I ever watched.

However, this election was completely different. All the ballot counters told me the exact same story, verbatim. And when I was using my binoculars, I confirmed what they were telling me. The ballot counters never checked for the authenticity of the ballots. They never checked the validity of the signature and did not even check to see if that person was eligible to vote or had already voted. A person could have had 1000 ballots to their name, and no one would have ever known. Plus, the counters were not looking at one ballot at a time. They were taking 3 to 4 ballots and just shoving them into the counting machine.

There was never any inspection or interrogation of the ballots. The quicker the ballots came to them, the quicker they would gather as many of them as they could hold and stuff them into the machine.

The whole thing was set-up the minute the ballots hit the convention center. Before the ballots were even brought to the counters, they were taken to a back room, out of sight, and removed from the bag. Then, the ballots were taken to these temps that had no election experience, who put them into these machines without even looking at them.

If anyone tells me that this election was not rigged, I will tell them that they are a complete liar. I was there. We all should be ashamed of what happened. I thought that I was in Russia or Venezuela watching the ballots get counted. This wasn't the election process of a free nation. This was what happens in a communist country.

I knew we weren't a communist nation, but I knew that's where we'd be heading if this were the way all future elections would be held.

There were lawyers there on the Trump team, and they did at least petition the courts to get us poll workers to closer to the counting. However, the closest we were ever allowed to be was only 6 feet from the counting. What was more ironic, was that when we began watching the poll counting from the new, designated 6-foot distance, the election officials started moving everything further away. The closer we got, the further they moved.

Hell, I was sometimes over 100 feet away from the counting at certain times. Days went on, and things did not get any better. "Our democracy is dead," was all that I could lament.

The whole process seemed liked a huge rush job. People were just feeding the counting machines nonstop. It was like a factory. Bags came in and ballots were stuffed as fast as they could fit into the counting machines. Looking back, I still ask myself the same question. "If it were such a rush job, why did counting stop in the middle of the first night?"

The Trump team quickly got wind that fraud was in the air and that Philadelphia was one of the hot spots. Because of the state's 20 critical electoral college votes, winning Pennsylvania could mean winning the election. As the days of counting continued, more and more people from the Trump team descended on the city. By the end of the week, Trump's political advisor, Corey Lewandowski, and "America's Mayor" himself, Rudy Giuliani, were now in Philadelphia.

On Friday, 3 days after election, I personally took Lewandowski aside and told him what was happening with the ballot counting. I told him that we should be protesting in the streets and informing the American people how the US election was being hijacked. It was fraud at its highest level. The integrity of the election had been compromised.

Little did I know at the time that this scam was just the tip of the iceberg. As days passed, it became apparent how certain ballot counting machines were automatically changing votes to Biden through their hacked Dominion software. Also, there were overvotes in some counties where there were more votes casted than people registered. There was also evidence that ballots voting for Biden were run through the counting machines multiple times, and many voters discovered when they went to the polls that someone had already voted for them. In addition, the tallies that were stored on memory sticks from the voting machines had their totals changed over the night.

Corey looked at me after I told him what I saw and asked me if I'd be willing to say something.

Hell yea I'd be happy to say something. To me, it didn't matter who won this damn election at this point. It was all about maintaining the integrity of the election itself. Without election integrity, our democracy is dead.

The next day lawyers from the Trump team picked me up from the Philadelphia Convention Center and took me to the Four Seasons Construction site. There, I met with Giuliani and told him the same story that I relayed to Lewandowski. Sitting side by side with the man, I went over every detail of what happened in Philadelphia.

While explaining everything to him, a young woman from his team walked in the room and informed him that the AP just called the election for Biden.

All was quiet as everyone there looked up, waiting for a response.

Giuliani curtly responded, "It doesn't matter. The AP, CNN and NBC don't pick the president."

It was very matter of fact and news did not faze him in the least. He knew it would just be a matter of time for the media to jump on the Biden-won bandwagon and call him the victor. As I said before, it just took 4 days for them to proclaim him the winner. The media didn't give a damn about election integrity or the possibility of voter fraud. They got their man into office any way they could, and that's all that mattered to them. Gore got his 37 days. President Trump was ousted in just 4 damn days.

And if you watched CNN after they called it for Biden, the screen always showed the election results. Day after day, it was in your face as if they wanted to beat it into American's psyche. It was like some sort of mental game that if people saw that Biden won enough times, even if the facts proved that he lost the election, they would not believe it.

Giuliani got up from the table, and things in the room became very rushed. I guess they wanted to get their press conference in before the news media lost interest and left. Because Biden was the projected winner, maybe they believed the different news organizations there would just pack up their bags and go. The election to them, though far from over, was finished in their minds.

As I walked over to the press conference, Giuliani asked me if I would give my name on national television.

Though it seemed like an easy question to answer, it was not for me. Giving my name and showing my face meant my entire past would be dug up once again. While in Philadelphia, I had started a new life and made new friends. Few knew of my previous conviction. Also, since it had been 25 years since the alleged event occurred, many people in Trenton either forgot about it or had just never heard that it happened. I knew by going up behind that podium a whole new can of worms was going to be released. However, instead of being on a local level, it was going to be broadcasted nationally.

My new reputation here in Philadelphia would be

lost. People would again be looking at me differently. Plus, the hate would return.

However, I knew this election was not about me. It was about our democracy and the American people. All I thought about was how many men and women died to give us a right to vote and preserve our freedom. I thought of all the sacrifices made by so many people to keep our country strong and nation safe. All these things made the decision easy.

I knew what I had to do.

The press conference began with a speech by Mayor Giuliani, while us poll watchers waited in the wings, anticipating our chance to speak on a national level. All I could think about the entire time was what would I say. The entire country would be looking at me.

As I was thinking, I heard Giuliani call my name.

"I'd like to introduce my friend Daryl," he said.

As the first poll worker to speak, I approached the podium and proudly gave my name. I was not going to hide. Consequences be damned.

My words came from the heart as I concisely recounted the travesty that occurred here in Philadelphia. After speaking my mind, I stepped away from the podium, knowing that I had done my duty as an American.

I have a picture of me speaking behind the podium.

Without your integrity, a man has nothing. Just like the time I would not admit to a crime that I never committed, I was not going to stay silent and do what people expected me to do. How could I face myself and my kids knowing that I had a chance to help save our country and did nothing about it? I wouldn't compromise myself now as I didn't compromise back in jail or during the parole hearings.

I had told the American people what I had seen, and I was proud that I had done so.

Chapter 11
Nelson Mandela Effect

The response I received for my action was swift and expected. However, what hurt me most was that it first came from my own people in Trenton. They were the ones who tipped off the news about my past. They were also the ones that told them I lived in Trenton and not in Philadelphia. I had been out of Trenton for 2 whole years. However, the truth never mattered to the media.

The hit for me was out.

The news media ran with it like wildfire. Not one of them even attempted to verify the story or call me for my point of view. If the people of Trenton said that I still lived there, that's all they needed to know. It didn't matter to them that I had lived in Philadelphia for 2 years and was a registered voter there. The story that I was a fraud met the media's narrative, and they ran with it.

Not only did the local Trenton newspapers and the media outlets run with the story, but the national news also crucified me every chance they got. The truth behind the voter fraud did not matter. Instead of looking for the facts, the media just wanted to villainize me and discredit my testimony.

It's like they were punishing me for telling the truth.

However, when did the truth matter to them? If it did, they would been investigating and reporting the massive voter fraud. Instead, they were more interested in the character assassination of an innocent man.

Are we living in Russia or Nazi Germany?

When did the mainstream media become the mouthpiece of the Democratic party?

My name was smeared on CNN, The View, NBC and by Bill Maher. The Daily Beast and NY Times also, among other papers, ran with the story. Some mentioned me by name. Others just showed my mug and sneered, "Look at Giuliani and his registered sex offender."

Not only were the news outlets out to get me, but regular people again began harassing me. I got death threats and constant harassment throughout all of social media.

I thought Facebook and Twitter had anti-hate filters and anti-racist filters that were supposed to flag hate speech. However, nothing was being flagged against me. All the hate flooded towards me, day after day. It was as if the filter amplified it my way.

I guess the filters don't work if you supported Trump or were a conservative. Try posting a story about election fraud and see how quickly that would have been taken down.

Plus, my new friends in Philadelphia all began looking at me different, and some even chose not to associate with me ever again. My longtime girlfriend also got harassed. Even her friends and family who didn't know about my past would contact her and ask why she is hanging out with a pervert and a sex offender. It made her upset, which upset me even more.

Though I had tried to start a new life, the media

crushed any hopes I had of forgetting the past. The stigma of a crime that I never committed would not leave.

As depression began to set in, the words of Dr. King once again revived my spirit.

God is still around. One day, you're going to need him. The problems of life will begin to overwhelm you; disappointments will begin to beat upon the door of your life like a tidal wave. And if you don't have a deep and patient faith, you aren't going to be able to make it.

Evil may so shape events that Caesar will occupy a palace and Christ on the cross, but one day that same Christ will rise up and split history into A.D. and B.C., so that even the life of Caesar must be dated by his name.

After inner prayer and listening to his words, the funk was quickly broken within a day. Let the people persecute me. Let the hate come on. However, I will stand tall and be the man God created me to be.

A little over a week after election day, I took a train down to Washington, DC for a pro-Trump rally. I felt like I needed to show my support for the president. I knew the election was stolen from him. I saw firsthand how the entire process had been rigged against both him and the American people.

Like me, most of the people who went down to DC felt disenfranchised and ripped off by the 2020 election. The system had failed us. It had failed all America.

At first, I was nervous about going to the rally. After being humiliated on national TV and in the major newspapers across the country, I honestly thought that I would be an outcast. I believed that even though these people agreed with me politically, they would cast me aside also.

It's not like it had not already happened. I was already getting the cold shoulder from friends and death threats from people around the country. Why would this place be any different?

When I got to the rally, I was overwhelmed with the amount of people there. Some estimated that there were already of 150,000 attendees. There was overwhelming support for the president and a feeling of comradery among everyone.

At first, I kept my head down, maintaining a low profile. However, I felt overwhelmed by the love and excitement of the people there. This was a true peaceful protest, not like the one reported by MSNBC's Ali Velshi as buildings were burning behind him.

The true activist inside me came alive. When I saw a man standing on a makeshift platform speaking in front of a massive crowd, I could not help myself. I'll be damned if anybody was going to silence me. I needed to speak my mind. The hell with the mainstream media and the hit they put on me.

When I got to the platform, one of the news reporters there instantly recognized me. "You are that poll worker from Philadelphia," he said as he pointed directly at me.

Proudly, I told him that it was me.

Instead of sneers and condemnation, he asked if I wanted to speak next.

"Hell, yes," I told him.

When I got up on the platform, I took the microphone and spoke my mind. I was not hiding from anybody. I told the large crowd that I was the poll worker who stood by Giuliani's side during the Philadelphia press conference. I told them that I was the first to speak out against this heinous criminal action committed by the Democratic party. The words came from my heart and flowed without hesitation. Below is a picture of me at this rally:

The crowd loved it. Instead of insults, I was met with cheers and smiles.

Overwhelmed by the support, I could feel a tear welling up in my eye. At that moment, any hesitation I had about speaking up against the election corruption instantly went away. I felt vindicated at that moment.

It was awesome!

After I spoke, people started coming up to me and calling me a national hero. I couldn't believe it. Also, people in the crowd wanted to take their pictures with me and were shaking my hand. This feeling of gratitude went on to follow me everywhere I went during the rally. It was like everyone there was an old friend that I hadn't seen for years. They all came up and greeted me as if we hadn't seen each other for years.

I felt stronger and more confident in myself than I did ever before. It was like I was Nelson Mandela. Though they locked him up in jail, they could not keep him down.

What was meant to harm him, only made him stronger.

I left the event with my faith in both people and humanity restored. America will survive as long as there are great, loving Americans like these living within her borders. I know the best days for both this great country and I lie ahead. Though the road may be rocky at times, it is the road that we all must follow to get to our God-given destiny.

With this faith we will be able to hew out of the mountain of despair, a stone of hope. With this faith we will be able to transform the jangling discords of our nation into a beautiful symphony of brotherhood. With this faith we will be able to speed up the day when all of God's children all over this nation - black men and white men, Jews and Gentiles, Protestants and Catholics will be able to join hands and sing in the words of the old negro spiritual, "Free at Last, Free at Last, Thank God Almighty, We are Free At Last.

-Dr. Martin Luther King Jr.

ABOUT THE AUTHOR
DARYL M. BROOKS

Daryl M. Brooks is a former three times U.S. Senate/Congressman candidate. On a historical note, he is the first African American from Trenton, NJ to run for Congress. Also he is the first person from Trenton, NJ to run for US Senate. He is the host of the On Fire Show. He has been featured in the New York Times, The Daily Beast, NY Daily News, USA Today, Twiggs Café Radio.com, PoliticIt.com, IQ 106.9 FM, Philly Channel 6, WZBN News 12, Comcast Newsmakers, NJN, Trentonian, Trenton Times, Star Ledger, National Korean Newspaper, Ernest Hancock on LRN,FM, the Philly Tribune and The Nubian News. Brooks is in the Library of Congress. He is rated in the top 100 on "Top Talk Radio Conservative Radio Host".

ABOUT THE AUTHOR
STEPHEN MARTINO

Stephen Martino is an Amazon bestselling author who has written the fast-paced *Alex Pella* novel series, which include *The New Reality, The Hidden Reality,* and *The Final Reality. The New Reality* became an Amazon bestseller and a winner of the 2020 New York City Big Book Distinguished Favorite, while *The Final Reality* went on to win a Gold medal for Thrillers at the FAPA awards and was a winner of the CYGNUS Book Awards for Science Fiction.

A member of the International Thriller Writers, Martino's action-political thrillers are often compared to such substantive novels as the *Sigma Series* by James Rollins, novels by Isaac Asimov, the *Da Vinci Code* by Dan Brown, and *The Andromeda Strain* by fellow physician, Michael Crichton.

His books have been featured on numerous blogs across the United States and Europe including *Indigo Quill, Writer's Life, Confessions of a Reader, As the Page Turns, I Heart Reading,* and *Mary's Cup of Tea* among others.

Martino's goal with his writing is to incorporate certain pressing topics that effect our word today such the unprecedented world-wide economic debt, globalism, the clash between East and West, and the growing schism in political interests with stimulating topics such as ancient Greek military history, biblical connections, medical twists, and futuristic scientific concepts.